Enriching Our Lives:

for Adult Literacy Teachers and Tutors
Poetry Lessons

FRANCIS E. KAZEMEK
St. Cloud State University
St. Cloud, Minnesota

PAT RIGG
American Language and Literacy
Tucson, Arizona

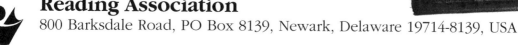

INTERNATIONAL Reading Association
800 Barksdale Road, PO Box 8139, Newark, Delaware 19714-8139, USA

Director of Publications   Joan M. Irwin
Assistant Director of Publications   Wendy Lapham Russ
Associate Editor   Christian A. Kempers
Assistant Editor   Janet Parrack
Production Department Manager   Iona Sauscermen
Graphic Designer   Boni Nash
Design Consultant   Larry Husfelt
Desktop Publishing Supervisor   Wendy Mazur
Desktop Publishing   Anette Schütz-Ruff
                       Cheryl Strum
Production Services Editor   David Roberts

Library of Congress Cataloging in Publication Data
Kazemek, Francis E.
    Enriching our lives: poetry lessons for adult literacy teachers and tutors/ Francis E. Kazemek, Pat Rigg.
        p.   cm.
    Includes bibliographical references (p.   ).
    1. Functional literacy—United States.   2. Poetry—Study and teaching (Adult education)—United States.   I. Rigg, Pat.   II. International Reading Association.   III. Title.
LC151.K39   1995   95-40495
808.1'071'5—dc20   CIP
ISBN 0-87207-137-5 (pbk.)

CONTENTS

INTRODUCTION

We both have worked for years with adult new writers and new readers, and we know from experience that poetry enriches our classes and our students. We believe it will enrich yours, too. In this handbook, we present nine detailed lessons, provide many examples of poetry for the adult classroom, explore different dimensions and features of poetry, and offer suggestions for further poetry reading and writing by you and your students.

Who Is This for?

This handbook is written for tutors who work with a single student and for adult basic education teachers who work with a class of adult new readers and writers. Throughout the book we address the different needs and concerns that these tutors and teachers have.

What's Here?

In this book there are nine sample lessons, each taking about 45 to 90 minutes in a literacy class. The lessons will vary in time according to your and your students' abilities, interests, and experience with poetry, and according to the dynamics of the particular classroom. Each lesson begins with the students' reading and writing a poem as a group, then suggests smaller group work, and ends with more individual composition and selection of reading.

We begin with a sample lesson in Chapter 1, which introduces the format and provides the basis for exploring the other sample lessons. In this first lesson on poetry about objects, you and your students read a poem about a cut apple, talk about and cut your own apples, and together create a group poem. The next chapter—"What's Poetic About

That?"—points out some poetic characteristics. The following chapters detail sample lessons, each of which focuses on a different type of poetry:

- poetry in conversation
- form poetry
- poetry as oral performance
- music as narrative poetry
- poetry about work
- lyric poetry
- found poetry
- humorous poetry

Each sample lesson can be expanded into several meetings, several lessons. We make a few suggestions but rely on you and your students to determine your own directions.

Because we recognize a common concern with such skills as spelling, punctuation, and some grammatical forms, we follow the sample lessons with a chapter of advice for dealing with these skills and include suggestions for incorporating computers and word processing in your poetry lessons.

The last chapter suggests some practical ways to make adult students' poetry known to a wider audience. Publishing of student writing is becoming more widespread; this chapter has some pointers for easy ways to do this.

Finally, we have provided a list of resources that will be helpful to those readers who are eager to further explore poetry with their students. We include a number of handbooks that nicely complement this one, books of poetry about work that can serve as extensions to Chapter 7, and a few collections that we like and have found useful.

What's Our View of Literacy?

We know that literacy is functional: people always have a reason to read or write. We read and write those things that apply to our lives, from the auto license renewal form to our grocery lists to holiday greetings. We never *practice* writing grocery lists, for example; we scribble one before we go shopping. If we buy a birthday card, the card is for a particular person, and we select one appropriate to that person's age and personality. In our teaching and in this handbook, we arrange the lessons to use both the functional and social nature of literacy.

We recognize that literacy is social: none of us reads or writes in a vacuum. We talk about what we're reading and writing. Listening to a friend recommend a book often makes us pick up that book at the library. After a heated discussion about current politics, we write our political representative or the editor of the local paper. Because literacy is social, the sample lessons in this book use group conversation as a means of supporting reading and writing. Therefore, we ask you and your students to join together into groups of four to six whenever possible. In these groups, you will listen to poems, talk about the poems, and together create your own poems.

We know that reading and writing share many characteristics and that each feeds the other. We learn a great deal about reading by writing; similarly, we learn how to write more clearly by reading. For example, an adult student with a rich knowledge of how Biblical language sounded (especially in the King James version of the Bible) dictated a part of the Sermon on the Mount following a language experience format; after he read his dictated version, which the instructor recorded, he could read the actual sermon with much greater confidence and ease. One of our students found a recipe with an attractive picture and wanted to know how to cook the dish. We helped her read the recipe, and the next week she dictated a recipe for her own version of the dish.

We believe that new readers should read and write the first day of class. We know that poetry is appropriate for the most beginning of literacy students.

What's Our Purpose?

Our purpose in this handbook is to help adult literacy teachers and students read and write poetry. Poetry helps us understand ourselves and our world; it helps us see ourselves and our world in new ways. At the same time, poetry lifts our language. We find ourselves using language in new ways, in ways that are more vivid, more powerful, and more fun. Poetry makes it clear that literacy is not just a set of mechanical skills for reading job advertisements or filling out applications.

Our poetry lessons with adults have always been successful, and we believe yours will be, too. Adult literacy students respond to literature with much intelligence and emotion. We hope you and your students enjoy these poetry lessons (and your own variations on them) as much as we have.

Chapter 1

POETRY ABOUT OBJECTS

Why Write About Objects?

We think it is important from the beginning to help our students see that poetry can be about the most commonplace things of life. It does not have to be abstract, vague, or confusing. Many of our students have had some negative experiences with poetry while in school. Because they couldn't read very well, the images and metaphors of poetry probably heightened their sense of frustration with written language. That's why, when we first mention poetry to our students, they often throw up their hands and exclaim, "Poetry? Oh, no, not me! I don't understand that stuff!"

We start with object poetry because it is comfortable for our students. Object poems tend to be short, are relatively easy to write, provide opportunities for looking closely at how language works, encourage discussion and social interaction, and are fun. Object poetry ties the language, images, and metaphors of poetry to the concrete things of everyday life. The language of poetry helps us see those everyday things in a fresh manner. And that's the power of literacy we want our students to experience: the ways that written language can make their lives richer, deeper, and more exciting.

Getting Ready

- Read through the complete lesson, and make estimates. How long do you think each activity will take with your particular students? Which students will work well together?

- Read the poem "The Apple" by Bruce Guernsey to yourself a couple of times, then read it aloud a few times, noting especially the last six lines, which are repeated after the full poem. You can't read a poem aloud too many times! The more you read it, the better you will appreciate it.

The Apple
by Bruce Guernsey

So this is the fruit that made us all human.
So this is the fruit we reached for and got.
So this is the fruit that ripens in autumn.

Cezanne,
I envy your eye.
Knowing roundness,
you put an apple in a bowl,
curve into curve
like lovers.

Mother,
you sliced the green ones for pie,
steaming like morning on the sill.

Doctor,
the apple I eat to keep you away
is the shape, the weight of a heart.

Long before the child, reaching up to pick,
before the ladder in the branches,
long before the tree, full in our yard,
a farmer rests
in the shade of his team.

Their dark sides shine.
In summer's last heat,
in the field's long work,
the apple he's saved
is cold on his teeth.

Shine an apple on your pants.
Make the apple genie dance.

(continued)

The Apple (continued)
by Bruce Guernsey

Rub him, rub him, into life.
Ask him for a pretty wife.

And for children I'd ask next,
talismans for the witch's hex.

One more wish is all that's left.
Beg him for eternal breath.

Quartered,

a seed rocks

in each tiny cradle.

Like blood,

in the air an apple

rusts.

———⬥⬥⬥———

Here are the final six lines of the poem again, which we use for this lesson:

Quartered,

a seed rocks

in each tiny cradle.

Like blood,

in the air an apple

rusts.

- Cut an apple in half lengthwise from the stem down. Then cut those halves in half lengthwise (quarter them as the final part of poem suggests). Those quarters will rock like a cradle when you set them skin side down on a surface.

Starting the Lesson

- Let the students in on your plans for this lesson. They can follow your instructions better if they know your objectives.

- Read the last six lines of "The Apple" aloud two or three times to the class. Then ask the students to read these lines aloud with you to create a kind of chorus. This rereading helps students appreciate the rhythm of the poem and makes it more understandable for even your most beginning student.

- Ask your students, "What do you think about these lines from this poem?" If you have only one student, be prepared to wait silently for some time until the student is convinced you really want to hear his or her opinion. (Practice waiting; 10 or 15 seconds are not very long, but they will seem so when you're sitting in silence with another person.) If you have several students, ask them to pair up and tell each other what they think. Pairing people reduces the chances of their "freezing" on you. If your whole class is unresponsive, move into the next step, which will focus attention on the apples.

> **Keep in Mind**
> It is important that each student have ample opportunity to create and voice an opinion. Many students will expect you to give your own opinion and will hesitate to voice theirs. This is to be expected; they have mistakenly learned that teachers have all the answers. It is through discussion that the students will create their own opinions.

- Cut an apple in half lengthwise as you did in the "Getting Ready" section, and show the students. Then cut it again so the apple is quartered. Give your students apples and knives. (Keep a few uncut apples for later.) You are giving them a chance to see those seeds rocking in cradles. The students' comments may be short, simple, and safe: "I like that." "That's nice." "Oh, now I see what it means."

- Discuss with your students whether they can see a seed rocking in a cradle. Did they ever see apple seeds that way before? Did you? Poetry can help us see more, see better, and see what we didn't see before. Has this poem helped you see the apple seeds in a new way?

- As the students look at the cut apples, ask if anyone sees the apple beginning to "rust." Again, has the poem helped you or your students to see apples differently? Had you ever compared a cut apple's discoloration to iron rusting before?

- Cut another apple in half horizontally. Does anyone mention the star shape that the seeds create? The poet didn't mention the star; when we see it, we are noticing something the poet either missed or chose not to write about in his poem.

- Read the last part of the poem aloud again. Are these poetry lines different for your students now that they have physically seen the seeds rocking in their cradles and the cut apple rusting? Ask the students to read the poem aloud with you.

> **Good Advice**
>
> If a student asks, "What's that word?" instead of reading the word, read the poem aloud again. We want students to understand that the individual word has meaning in a complete context; we always want them to have a meaningful experience with the poem and not simply read for word identification. (See Chapter 11 "What About Skills?" for more ideas about dealing with such issues.)

Writing Poetry

Getting Particular

Ask your students to find out more about the apple pieces they have in front of them. Hold one in the palm of a hand: What are the sensations of touch? Is it cool? How heavy is it? What are the textures? Does it remind you of anything else (as the discoloration reminded the poet of rusting)? Sniff the apple piece: How does it smell? Do the odors remind you of anything? Peel off some skin. Put a slice on your tongue: How does it taste? Take a bite from another piece: how does it sound?

If you are tutoring one student, the two of you can do these things together, but the advantage of working in bigger groups is that it is easier to generate more ideas.

As the students investigate the apples, write what they say on a large sheet of newsprint or the chalkboard. Listen for expressions about tactile sensations, visual impressions, odors, and tastes, and listen for comparisons. Chances are, you will get both literal impressions about the senses and expressions such as, "The uncut apple is like a small red world," "The blossom end looks like a bomb," or "There's a star in the middle when you cut it."

These comparisons—similes and metaphors—join two different things, and it is this combination that helps us see both the two things differently. Such figurative language is at the heart of poetry. A star in the sky and a star in the center of a cut apple are quite different things; calling the pattern in the cut apple a "star" makes our view of the apple richer at the same time that it opens possibilities for seeing stars in the sky differently. Of course, you don't have to spend class time talking about this because adults already instinctively know this and you and your students will find it more enjoyable to *do* poetry (read and write poems) than to talk about it. In fact, we've learned from our students that talking about similes, metaphors, and other figurative language will not only get in the way of the poetry but may bring back unpleasant school memories for some adults.

While you are writing the students' ideas on newsprint or the chalkboard, the students are learning to read these ideas because the context is so clear: they know what others are talking about, so they can read what others dictate. It is helpful for everyone, especially your beginning literacy students, if you repeat what students dictate as you write it and after you write it, asking if you have correctly written what the students said. You may miss something, or they may change their minds about their ideas.

Forming a Group Poem

When the students are out of ideas, or when you have a long list (say, 15 to 25 descriptions) on the board, suggest a group poem be made by selecting and rearranging some of the items listed. The same process you have been following continues: the students decide what goes where, and you write as they tell you. Here's an example of a list we brainstormed containing both literal and figurative expressions:

> red, sweet, like sugar, smooth, waxy, red face with light freckles, white flesh, star-heart, crunching sound, tiny explosion when bitten, autumn on the tongue, made for apple-bobbing, stem like a fuse, naked and waiting for a coat of caramel, thin-skinned, pregnant with quadruplets inside, unsteady on its feet

Here are the short poems we formed based on the list:

Untitled
Red-faced and freckled,
sweet, swollen
with quadruplets,
unsteady on her feet.

Biting an Apple
The explosion
releases autumn,
Halloween bobbing,
and the taste of caramel
stuck to the teeth.

When your students are shaping the items from their list into a poem, it is important to foster an atmosphere of acceptance, tentativeness, and openness in which language play and dialogue are utmost. You and your students should have *fun* playing with words and images. Encourage students to build on and bounce off others' ideas. Suggest that they write a few poems using different items from their list. There is nothing wrong with your participating in the poem making, but limit your contribution to one word or phrase. The students should feel that the poem is theirs, not yours.

It is important for you to read the students' work aloud. When writers get a chance to hear their work in someone else's voice, it can give them a new perspective on their own creation. More important, the teacher makes it clear that this work is valuable; it is worth the teacher's time, attention, effort and in the teacher's opinion, worth class time, attention, and effort.

Making Connections

Poetry about objects is fun to read and write. Once students become familiar with the style of these poems, they like to write a lot of them. Bring in different object poems and share one each class meeting. Later lessons might once again be done as a whole class, but they might also involve small-group or individual writing. The kinds of objects you and your students can write about are countless. As an immediate follow-up lesson to the apple poem, we suggest bringing to class a worn shoe to use as an object. Your students might want to bring in items that clearly have a history, for example, a wedding veil, antique kettle, or ashtray. The students can focus on these personal items as a class or as small groups or individuals. Chapter 4, "Form Poetry," ties in nicely with writing about objects.

Students can begin to save in personal poetry folders their object poems and the other poetry they write in and out of class. These folders do not need to be elaborate; simple file folders will do. Such collections give students a sense of pride and accomplishment, and they provide a rich source for continued reading, writing, and sharing.

Last, encourage your students who have children to write object poems at home. This is fun for both adults and children and fosters meaningful literacy use in the home setting. Ask them to bring in and share the object poems they write at home.

Summing Up

Reading and writing poetry about objects is a pleasant, nonthreatening way to introduce poetry to your students. Group writing of object poems fosters cooperation and imagination and allows students to talk about and look closely at how written language works and how poems are put together. In addition to demonstrating to your students the power of literacy in helping us see the world differently, writing object poetry builds your students' sense of themselves as creative language users, as budding poets.

Chapter 2

WHAT'S POETIC ABOUT THAT?

"What's poetic about an apple seed or an apple rotting?" Is that what your students are asking? In this chapter, we want to address this question and related questions that your students may bring up as they begin to read and write more poetry, such as "What makes something poetic?" "What's poetry good for?" "Why spend time on it?" "What subjects are appropriate for poetry?" "Does poetry have to rhyme?" "Do poems have to be a certain length?" and "How can I learn more about poetry?"

The apple poem from the lesson on object poetry offers a fine example for dealing with these questions. Let's look at the final part of the poem again:

The Apple
by Bruce Guernsey

Quartered,
a seed rocks
in each tiny cradle.

Like blood,
in the air an apple
rusts.

—⟨∞⟩—

(From Blair & Ketchum's *Country Journal*, August 1980 and October 1981. Copyright 1980 by Country Journal Publishing Co., Inc. Reprinted by permission of the publisher and Bruce Guernsey.)

What Makes Something Poetic?

Form is our first clue that this is a poem, not a piece of prose. The careful balancing of stanzas, words, images, and rhythms would be greatly lost if we changed this part of "The Apple" to read: "When an apple is quartered, a seed rocks in each tiny cradle. Like blood in the air, an apple rusts." The form helps us hear and understand the poem's ideas and images by giving greater emphasis to certain expressions that would not be as apparent in prose form.

We don't want to dissect the poem to death, because we (and you) have suffered through that in more than one class, so we will point out only a few ways in which the form helps us read and understand the poem. In the second stanza of this part of the poem, the words at the end of the lines are "blood, apple, rusts." Because those words are at the end of their lines they receive a little more stress than the other words, so readers sense the slightly greater importance of these. One more example: in the first stanza, the first line is one word—"quartered"— but that one word stands for something like "When an apple is cut into fourths, or is quartered." The poet alerts us to the weight of "quartered" by putting the word by itself. The best way of appreciating the form of a poem is to read it aloud several times and to experiment with different ways of emphasizing words and connecting lines.

What's Poetry Good for? Why Spend Time on It?

The purpose of poetry is to enlarge our lives. It helps us see the world and other people in all their complexity and possibility. We usually don't think of an apple in terms of blood or of its rusting. Now that we've read this poem, we can never again cut open an apple without seeing and thinking of seeds rocking in cradles.

Poetry also enlarges our lives through the pleasure it gives us and the joy and excitement we feel when we read it, hear it, talk about it, and relate it to our own lives. If a particular poem doesn't move us in some way, then we should look to another one. There is no poem that will give pleasure to all people. However, sometimes we need to read and hear a poem many times, think about it for a while, and discuss it with others before we come to appreciate it. Our first reaction is not always our fullest.

What Subjects Are Appropriate for Poetry?

We built the lesson on object poetry around a poem about apples to highlight the fact that poetry does not have to be about obscure, abstract, or grandiose subjects such as "Love," "Truth," "Beauty," and so forth. Most poetry deals with little loves, truths, and beauties. It focuses on the particulars of everyday life, the daily instances and expressions of love and beauty. The most commonplace things of life—an apple, for example—are fit subjects for poetry.

Before you move on to the lessons in the following chapters, try reading aloud several times the poem "homage to my hair" by Lucille Clifton. We think you will better see and hear what we've been talking about.

homage to my hair
by Lucille Clifton

when i feel her jump up and dance
i hear the music! my God
i'm talking about my nappy hair!
she is a challenge to your hand
Black man,
she is as tasty on your tongue as good greens
Black man,
she can touch your mind
with her electric fingers and
the grayer she do get, good God,
the Blacker she do be!

—⟋⟋⟋—

(From *two-headed woman* by Lucille Clifton. Copyright 1980 by University of Massachusetts Press. Reprinted by permission of Curtis Brown, Ltd.)

Does Poetry Have to Rhyme?

One poem many people in the United States know by heart is Joyce Kilmer's "Trees" (I think that I shall never see / A poem lovely as a tree...), and many assume that any poem should have a similar form. But poetry does not have to rhyme. The poems we have already shared with you as examples do not have heavy rhymes at the ends of lines. In that respect they are quite different from poetry you may have studied or even memorized in school, such as the following lines from Eugene Field's "Little Boy Blue."

The little toy dog is covered with dust,
But sturdy and staunch he stands;
And the little toy soldier is red with rust,
And his musket moulds in his hands.

Poems can have various sorts of rhymes and plays with the sounds of language, some of which we will discuss in more detail in later lessons. For now, we just want to assure you that your students do not have to make their poems rhyme. As a matter of fact, we suggest that you and your students try writing without rhyme for a while. Many beginning writers with whom we have worked have blocked themselves by focusing on form rather than on purpose; we've seen beginning poets strain, skew, and strangle their sentences and their sense—just to get a rhyme. As this last sentence full of alliteration shows, you can play with the sounds of language without letting the sound overcome the sense, if you don't demand rhyme.

Do Poems Have to Be a Certain Length?

No, they do not. Langston Hughes has a wonderfully succinct poem with a title almost as long as the poem:

Little Lyric (Of Great Importance)
by Langston Hughes

I wish the rent
Was heaven sent.

—◦◦◦—

(From *Selected Poems by Langston Hughes.* Copyright 1942 by Alfred A. Knopf, Inc. Reprinted by permission of the publisher.)

On the other hand, John Milton's *Paradise Lost* and Tennyson's *Idylls of the King* are hundreds of pages long.

How Can I Find Out More About Poetry?

The best way to find out about poetry is to read a wide variety of it, preferably several times aloud. Give it a chance to soak in. Our experiences with different poems will give us the internal touchstones that let us recognize poetry in the conversation of those around us and respect the work of long-dead poets. The more of it we read, the better we know it.

Chapter 3

POETRY IN CONVERSATION

Is There Poetry in Conversation?

The poet Carl Sandburg said that people often talk poetry without being aware of it. If you take time to listen closely to people talking in a variety of situations, we think that you will agree. Eavesdrop in a popular coffee shop some morning and listen to the banter among the regular customers, servers, and cooks. Listen to a couple of teenagers with greasy knuckles and nails talk about the engines of their "hot" cars. Let a group of gardeners talk to you about flowers while having tea and cookies. Pay attention to the words, expressions, and images that elderly people use when they are trying to outdo one another with "hard times" stories from their youth.

Poems using conversation help students make the connections between the language they use and hear every day and that of poetry. Such poems further demystify the nature of poetry and the poet as belonging to some other-worldly sphere. A typical response from students who first hear a number of conversation poems is, "Hey, I can do that." Further, being literate means being more aware of language and how it is used to inform, persuade, threaten, console, compliment, and so on. Conversation poems help students tune in to language; they become more attentive listeners and more sophisticated readers and writers.

Getting Ready

- Read through the lesson.
- Practice reading "Canción Tonta/Silly Song" by Federico García Lorca aloud. (If you don't speak Spanish but have a student who does, ask him or her to help you.) Because this is a conversation poem,

you may want to decide how you will distinguish between the two speakers. Many oral readers just shift direction, looking to the left for one speaker, to the right for the other. Some oral readers will change the volume and pitch of their voice for each speaker.

Cancíon Tonta	Silly Song
by Federico García Lorca	

Mamá, Yo quiero ser de plata.	Mama, I wish I were silver.
Hijo, tendrás mucho frío.	Son, You'd be very cold.
Mamá, Yo quiero ser de agua.	Mama, I wish I were water.
Hijo, tendrás mucho frío.	Son, You'd be very cold.
Mamá, Bórdame en tu almohada.	Mama, Embroider me on your pillow.
¡Eso sí! ¡ Ahora mismo!	That, yes! Right away!

(From *The Selected Poems of Federico García Lorca.* Copyright 1952 by New Directions Publishing Corp. Reprinted by permission of New Directions Publishing Corp.)

- Try your hand at writing a conversation poem between yourself and your mother or other close relative, following this pattern. You already know how important we think it is for you to be writing the same thing as your students and at the same time. We also think a little practice ahead of time can help you get a sense of what your students will be attempting.

  Here are a few poems that we wrote patterned on "Silly Song." Instead of mother to son, we've tried mother to daughter and father to son.

  Mama,
  I wish I were iron.
     Daughter,
     You'd rust.

Mama,
I wish I were fire.
  Daughter,
  You'd burn up.
Mama,
Hold me in your locket!
  That, yes!
  Right away!

Mama,
I wish I were gold.
  Daughter,
  You'd be too soft.
Mama,
I wish I were air.
  Daughter,
  You'd be lonely.
Mama,
Carry me in your purse.
  That, yes!
  Right away!

Papa,
I wish I were coyote.
  Son,
  You'd be too sad.
Papa,
I wish I were eagle.
  Son,
  You'd be too proud.
Papa,
Carry me on your back.
  That, yes!
  Right away!

The language of everyday rituals, such as bidding a friend good-bye or a family member good night, often is poetic in its repetition, strong rhythm, and frequent rhyme. Once again, we can feel and hear the rhythm of poetry in our daily language by repeating a conversational exchange as simple and commonplace as this one:

"See ya 'round."
"Yeah, see ya."

or this:

"See you later, alligator!"
"After a while, crocodile!"

or this one:

"Good night, sleep tight."
"Don't let the bed bugs bite!"

Starting the Lesson

- Explain to your students what you'll be doing together in the lesson. Emphasize the fact that poetry can come from the most common, everyday situations and that you'll be writing and reading poetry to prove it.

- Brainstorm with your students different ways of saying good-bye. List them on the chalkboard or on newsprint. Be prepared with a few suggestions if students are reticent and you need to get things going. Try to get a list of 10 to 15 good-byes. This should be easy to do with a class. If you are tutoring a single student, then both of you will have to work a little harder.

- After the students appear to be out of ideas, ask them to select the good-byes they consider the wittiest and those they consider the most poetic (rhythmic and repetitive). Write these on a different section of the board or on a fresh piece of newsprint. Ask the students to read these two or three exchanges aloud: half the group read one line, the other half read the response. Reread each exchange a couple of times.

- If the students and you are having fun and want to continue this process, try good nights or greetings ("Hi, what's happenin'?" "Not much. What about you?") and brainstorm, select, and read aloud. This rereading of material students already generated and discussed is not just fun; the repetition makes that material easily readable, even to the most beginning reader.

- Read "Canción Tonta/Silly Song" aloud to the class a few times. Share with them the poem and have them follow along as you read it again.

- Divide the class in half and have the students read the poem aloud with you, one half of the class taking the mother's part, and the other half the son's. If you have Spanish speakers in class, they can teach the other students how to read it in Spanish.

Please Note

People who speak only English may ask why a Spanish version of a poem is included in this lesson. We included it because it is the original version of the poem; the English version is a translation. We also enjoy the look and sound of Spanish, even though neither of us can read or speak the language. Listening to the sounds of language in meaningful poems, whether they are in Spanish or English, will help your students naturally develop an ear for language in a manner that all the phonics workbook pages can never duplicate. If some of your students speak Spanish as their first language, maybe they can explain the poem's appeal in Spanish or how the poem's meaning changes in the translation to English.

- Ask your students to talk to one another by asking, "What do you think?" As we mentioned in the lesson on the apple poem, it is important that your students try out their ideas through talk, rather than sit waiting to hear what you think. Once in a while your students may choose not to discuss the poem with others. They may not have yet formed a sense of community with one another in the class; they may feel they don't understand the poem well enough to discuss it.

Good Advice

What can you do if your students freeze? Remember that with the apple poem, we suggested that if the class was reticent to speak, you could focus attention on the object itself. In this lesson, we suggest that you now focus attention on silly exchanges, preferably between parent and child. You could start with the prompts, "Do you remember any time you and your parent had a silly conversation?" "What did each of you say?" or "Do you and your own children ever have similar conversations?"

Another option is to role-play the poem. Have students discuss where and when this exchange might take place. Then have them pair up: one role-play the mother, the other the son.

- Give your students a chance to share their observations and questions with one another. It is important that each person feel free to guess the poem's meanings. Talking about those guesses and rereading a line or two to support those guesses are the ways each person learns about the poem and about reading.

Writing Poetry

For this lesson, tell the students they can use "Canción Tonta/ Silly Song" as a pattern for writing their own conversation poems with their family members. Of course, no one has to use the pattern, and no one has to use a mother-son conversation. You can share the mother-daughter and father-son poems we wrote and perhaps the one you wrote before the lesson. Those who see the poem's pattern as a support for their own poem, however, are invited to use it.

Ask students to pair up and talk about a conversation they want to write as a poem. Give them time to talk. This talking is a vital and necessary part of writing. After partners have had a chance to talk about conversations that they might use as poems, ask them to write them. Depending on the abilities of your students, you can have individuals write their own poems, partners work together on one or two poems, or you can assist the beginning, tentative writers. You want to foster a lot of talk and collaboration among the students as they are writing. Tell them they might want to read parts of their poems to others as they are writing them.

As the students are finishing their work, tell them that those who want to share their conversation poems will be able to do so at the next class meeting. Ask them if you can then copy the final versions for inclusion in a class poetry book.

Making Connections

In this lesson you and your class focused on good-byes and silly talk between mother and son. As a follow-up activity, ask students to bring in examples of poetic conversations they've heard at work, on the street, or at home. They can use their memories or write what they hear in a pocket notebook.

You can also encourage those students with children at home to try to write conversation poems. They and their children can first talk out a silly conversation and then write it. Ask them to bring these poems to class and share them.

If you and your students have enjoyed this lesson and would like to continue with conversation poetry, you can repeat the process with greetings or with the conversation poems your students bring in.

Other conversation poems that you might want to read and share with your students include Langston Hughes's "Mother to Son," William Carlos Williams's "At the Bar," and Robert Frost's "The Death of the Hired Man." Paul Fleischman's book *Joyful Noise: Poems for Two Voices*, which we use in a later lesson on oral performance, has some fine two-part poems. Your public library will have all these works. Ask your librarian if you need help locating a particular book or poem.

Summing Up

The more you can help your students connect their own language to that of poetry, the more confidence they will develop as readers and writers of poems. If you and your students pay special attention to the everyday language around you, you will have a wealth of resources from which to write individual, partner, small-group, and whole-class poems.

Chapter 4

FORM POETRY

Form poetry offers structures for new writers into which they can insert their own words. The different forms may look like fill-in-the-blank exercises that students had for years in school, but form poetry is a lot more fun and a great deal more meaningful than those exercises. Writing a poem about oneself, for example, can be an enjoyable and purposeful class activity.

Form poetry gives new writers a sense of support, and it allows them to complete a poem fairly fast. However, the major disadvantages of such structures for new writers include a restriction of both form and thought, a surface treatment of ideas, and limited grammatical and poetic structure (for example, lack of complete sentence structure, rhyme, and repetition).

Getting Ready
- Read through the complete lesson.
- Try writing at least one or more of each of the form poems we describe. We present some common types of form poetry that we have found to be successful with adult readers and writers. Play with and enjoy them. You and your students could spend a full 10 weeks on form poetry, if that appeals to you and them.

Starting the Lesson
We suggest that you follow a similar lesson format, as follows, for all the types of form poems described.
- Tell your students that there are various, fairly easy ways of writing poetry. Present to them the form poetry you are using, and let them follow along as you read the example poem(s) a couple of times.
- Ask your students to discuss what they notice about the particular form. For example, is the poem written as a list? Does it have a cer-

tain number of words per line, as in a cinquain poem? Through this class discussion highlight the form of the poem.

- Next, try writing one or more of these form poems together as a class. Brainstorm some possible topics and list them on the board or a sheet of newsprint. Select one topic and then brainstorm possible words and phrases that will fit into the form. Write them on the board and read and reread them with the whole class. Depending on the type of poem, have students work in pairs, small groups, or as individuals and write their own. Circulate and offer encouragement and assistance.

- After students have written their own poems, share them with the rest of the class. Be sure to point out the particular form and ways in which it can be (and most likely will be) played with and modified.

- Encourage students with children to write such form poems with them at home. Tell them to bring in and share any of the poems written at home.

Alphabet Poems

Sometimes a list of items can be a poem, even though at first it looks like a grocery list someone might jot before a trip to the grocery store, for example. One such list is the alphabet poem. An example of an alphabet poem that students can use to introduce one another is the autobiographical list, using the letters of one's name as the initial letters of a word for each line:

> **Y**oung
> **O**ld-fashioned
> **U**seful
> **R**eader
>
> **N**ewcomer
> **A**unt
> **M**other
> **E**lder

This list does not have to be limited to one word per line; students can create phrases to describe themselves, as in the following example:

> **Y**oung in heart
> **O**ld-fashioned in dress
> **U**seful in the kitchen
> **R**eader of novels

Writing Poetry

Newcomer to class
Aunt of nephews
Mother of two
Elder sister

After students are acquainted, they can write alphabet poems about one another, perhaps working in pairs so they have a chance to talk before putting pen to paper. When the name is longer than five letters, they can use a nickname or alter the form itself to accommodate more lines, perhaps doubling the lines of description. Here's an example by Pat:

Francis
Reader Runner
Asker Listener Learner
Night owl Bookworm
Kazemek

Alphabet poems do not have to be restricted to names; they can be written about anything. Another use of alphabet poems is to write them for special occasions, for example, birthdays, Mother's and Father's Days, holidays, and so forth. They lend themselves to a greeting card format. (See the chapter on publishing for suggestions on using the computer to produce greeting cards.) A Christmas card might begin as follows:

Merry
Elves
Ring
Round
You

As mentioned, the alphabet poem has some disadvantages for new literacy students: there is no sentence structure, no grammar to give clues to the reader, and no support from the rhyme and repetition of other kinds of poetry. For groups creating alphabet poems on newsprint or the board, or for pairs working together, this disadvantage is not great. The alphabet poem is especially appropriate for a tutor working with one student.

List Poems

List poems are similar to alphabet poems, except that they do not rely on the alphabetic structure. They simply describe something by compiling a long or short list related to that person or thing. List poems and list poem elements have been used in both traditional and contemporary poetry. The poet William Carlos Williams included a grocery list in one of his long poems. The repetition of the word *begat* in the beginning of the *New Testament* ("Abraham begat Isaac, and Isaac begat Jacob, and Jacob begat Judah and his brothers...") is another example.

List poems tend to be easier to write than alphabet poems because the lines are not controlled by particular letters. Each line can begin with any letter and can be of any length. Like alphabet poems, they can be written on any subject. List poems are fun to write as a whole class because the more ideas that are brainstormed, the longer the list usually becomes. Here's an example of the start of a list poem:

Coyotes
Hounded, trapped, tortured, and killed
Desert dwellers and hunters
Survivors across the land
Singers in the night-time
Magic-makers and shape-shifters
Tricksters and story-tellers
...and so on

Cinquain Poems

A cinquain is a five-line poem that can be written about almost any topic. The pattern is easy to follow:

Line 1	one word	gives the title or name of the subject
Line 2	two words	describes the subject in line 1
Line 3	three words	describes an action of the subject
Line 4	four words	expresses a feeling of the subject or a feeling you have about it
Line 5	one word	renames the subject in line 1

Here's an example of a cinquain poem:

Cicada
ugly noisy
thrumming sawing praying
sad frightened regretful lonely
singer

Cinquains are fun to write as a whole group and as individuals. When working with a whole group, most often so many ideas are coming from the students that we have them compose two or three cinquains simultaneously (while we write quickly on the board!). When students are working on their own cinquain or writing one with a partner, we suggest that they refer to a beginning-level thesaurus if they'd like. This gets them in the habit of using reference books and also encourages them to explore and play with the words and sounds of the language.

The cinquain is also another form poem that lends itself to occasional verse—that is, cards for birthdays, holidays, greetings, and so on. For example, a Mother's Day cinquain might look like this:

Mom
beautiful feisty
caring supporting sharing
I love you so
Helen

Haiku Poems

Haiku (the same word is used for both singular and plural) is a short two-to-four line poem that tries to capture an instant in time, a moment of insight. Haiku generally deal with the flashes of insight or inspiration that you might have as you walk in a park or woods or as you look out into your backyard in the early morning.

Many people believe that haiku must follow a three-line, 5-7-5 syllable format. Your students who have spent any time in school will probably remember teachers trying to get them to find words that fit the syllable requirements of each line. We strongly recommend *not* writing haiku in this fashion. A focus on the number of syllables often results in undue attention to the form rather than to the creation of an interesting poem. Moreover, this focus on syllables is often frustrating to people who are not proficient readers and writers.

We encourage you to share with your students haiku examples from the Japanese masters (there are many collections of such poetry) and haiku-like poems from other writers. On the next page are two examples from the Japanese masters.

Untitled

by Issa

Grasshopper,
Do not trample to pieces
The pearls of bright dew.

Untitled

by Buson

A flash of lightning!
The sound of dew
Dripping down the bamboos.

(Both from *Haiku*, edited and translated by
R.H. Blyth. Reprinted by permission of The
Hokuseido Press.)

Here are two haiku-like poems from American poets:

Splinter

by Carl Sandburg

The voice of the last cricket
across the first frost
is one kind of good-by.
It is so thin a splinter of singing.

(From *Good Morning, America*. Copyright
1928 and renewed 1956 by Carl Sandburg.
Reprinted by permission of Harcourt Brace
& Company.)

Chinese Nightingale

by William Carlos Williams

Long before dawn your light
Shone in the window, Sam Wu;
You were at your trade.

—◦◦◦—

Haiku encourage students to open themselves to the world around them, to listen, look, smell, taste, and feel. The writing of haiku acknowledges insight and inspiration, whether it is in looking closely at a grasshopper on a dew-covered leaf or seeing a lone light in a shop window before dawn. Students can write haiku alone or together by remembering and talking about experiences and insights in the past, looking at and discussing nature pictures and photographs (a collection of pictures from *National Geographic* and other nature-wildlife magazines are especially helpful when writing haiku), or exploring closely a particular nature object, for example, a handful of seashells, a flower, a gnarled branch, a stone, and so forth. Writing haiku about objects can be connected to the object poetry writing described in Chapter 1.

Crazy Poems

Crazy poems are deliberate nonsense. A group brainstorms all the odd words they can think of, and these are listed on newsprint or the board. Then pairs of students or individuals select and arrange these into a crazy poem, something that sounds as though it should make sense but doesn't. Here's an example of a brainstormed list we made:

succulent	virtuoso	pickled	nefarious
onomatopoeia	languish	equila	rococo
nincompoop	rigmarole	plop	feckless
roly-poly	galumphing	snorkel	baroque
mellifluous	gregarious	chic-chi	Delbert

Here's the crazy poem that we wrote as we sat around and laughed:

> Succulent virtuosos languish
> by rococo roly-polys.
> Plop! Gregarious baroques
> galumphed past Delbert.
> "Equila! Equila! Equila!"
> pickled nincompoops snorkel,
> mellifluously call:
> "Equila! Equila! Equila!"

Crazy poem writing fosters the sense of play with language that we believe is so important in adult literacy programs. Crazy poetry also helps students play with the relationships between letters and sound (phonics) and is another instance in which the thesaurus becomes a useful tool. Last, this is the kind of enjoyable poetry writing that children love to fool around with. Encourage your students with children at home to write crazy poems and share some of them with the class.

The reading and writing of crazy poetry is easier and more fun if done with a whole class or at least a small group. The more people are sharing and acting silly the better! Crazy poems can be written by a tutor and student; however, as tutor, be sure that you foster and demonstrate the kind of openness and silliness necessary for such poetry.

Making Connections

We have already described how the different types of form poetry connect to other lessons in this handbook. In addition, form poetry allows students to make connections with their children at home. The fun that adults and children have writing form poetry helps foster intergenerational literacy.

Summing Up

You can promote poetry reading and writing by providing students with different structures that make it easy. You can also encourage attention to the wealth of the English vocabulary by having students read and write poetry that highlights the word rather than any particular grammatical structure.

Chapter 5

POETRY AS ORAL PERFORMANCE

Why Oral Performance?

We have emphasized reading poems aloud to students more than once because one important characteristic of poetry is how it *sounds*. In this lesson, we want to focus on that characteristic. Some poems have such strong rhythms and repetitions that they can and should be performed—that is, accompanied by physical movements such as hand clapping, arm waving, or dancing. We want you to enjoy some activities that involve you and your students as performers. The poems here cannot be read silently; they must be read aloud, and they need to be acted out in some way.

This lesson requires that there be a sense of community in the class: without it, students who are strangers will not perform for one another. If your students work well together and have already formed a community, this lesson can increase that bond: people who feel comfortable with one another are willing to perform, and through performing the poem "Water Boatmen" together, they become more relaxed and ready to create a new performance with their own poetry.

Getting Ready

• Read "Water Boatmen" by Paul Fleischman several times aloud. If possible, practice reading it as a conversational poem with someone else. It is ideal if one of your students and you can practice the poem together before you bring it to class.

Water Boatmen
by Paul Fleischman

"Stroke!"	"Stroke!"
We're water boatmen	
"Stroke!"	"Stroke!"
	up early, rowing
"Stroke!"	"Stroke!"
We're cockswain calling	
"Stroke!"	"Stroke!"
	and oarsmen straining
"Stroke!"	"Stroke!"
and six-man racing shell	
rolled into one.	
	We're water boatmen
"Stroke!"	"Stroke!"
worn-out from rowing	
"Stroke!"	"Stroke!"
	bound for the bottom
"Stroke!"	"Stroke!"
of this deep millpond	
"Stroke!"	"Stroke!"
	where we arrive
and shout the order	
"Rest!"	"Rest!"

(From *Joyful Noise: Poems for Two Voices* by Paul Fleischman. Copyright 1988 by Paul Fleischman. Reprinted by permission of HarperCollins Publishers.)

This poem helps us see two things at once—insects swimming under water and people rowing a racing shell on top. As we have mentioned earlier, this is one of the main reasons we have poetry: it can help us to see more, see differently, and see better. The vision this poem offers is rich in that it does not let us see just a crew of six men rowing, or just bugs swimming to the bottom of a pond, but both at once—like the star in the apple, like the apple seed being a baby apple rocking in its cradle. The shell of this insect with six legs looks like a racing shell with six oars, and the movement of the insect legs is like the movement of human arms rowing—both at once.

- As you look at this poem, note the number of unfamiliar words. The word "stroke" appears 18 times, and the poem will teach the word, if you and the students act it out as you read the poem aloud. A few of the other terms such as "cockswain," "oarsmen," "millpond," "racing shell," and "water boatmen" will be known to people who row or know something about rowing. Some of these are self-explanatory, even to land lubbers: "millpond" and "oarsmen," for example. We think the poem teaches its readers that a cockswain calls and oarsmen strain to row to the beat the cockswain calls. Maybe some students have rowed before, perhaps fishing or on some camp outing; did they ever have someone in the boat call out "Pull!" or "Row faster!"? That's the kind of thing a cockswain does with the water boatmen. (By the way, we looked up the pronunciation of cockswain and found it had two equally acceptable pronunciations: cock + swain and cock + sun.) Another minor aside: this poem is particularly rich in compound words; in addition to the ones just listed are "six-man" and "worn-out."

- Assemble newsprint, markers, tape, and any other materials that you'll need in class.

Starting the Lesson

- If you work with several people, ask someone, preferably one of your best readers, to act out the poem with you. Again, it is ideal if you and the student are able to practice before class, but that is not always possible. Write "Stroke!" on the board, and ask your class to say that as a chorus each time you and the student pull on those imaginary oars. (Extend your arms straight out in front of you, close your hands into fists as though you were grasping an oar, and pull both hands to your chest as you say "Stroke!") Even the most beginning reader can join with classmates in saying "Stroke!" Go through the poem two or three times this way, without showing the other students the poem.

Please Note

If you are a tutor with only one student, many of the suggestions will be more difficult than if you work with at least two or three other people. Perhaps another tutor and student can join you for this and the next lesson. If it's only the two of you, you may want your student to join you in the "Stroke!" lines: that is, you read the other lines, then you and your student say "Stroke!" as you both imitate an oarsman.

- Ask your students, "What pictures do you see?" "Who here has rowed?" "What about those bugs?" Get the students talking about their experience rowing; get them talking about the images they have of rowers, racing shells, and water bugs of different sorts. Give them time to think, talk, and compare information and images.

- When it appears that they're running out of ideas, show your students the poem.

- Divide the class in half, and the two of you who performed the poem now lead the class in their performing: half the class can read with you, half with your assistant. Everyone comes in on the chorus, and everyone physically rows when "Stroke!" is read.

- Ask students to think about expressions they hear almost daily on the street, at work, among friends, and so on that compare people to insects or somehow relate people and insects. As the students brainstorm these, you can write them on newsprint or on the board. Some words you'll hear (or need to have ready yourself as starters) include "busy as bees," "antsy" (impatient), "drone," "gadfly," "bug," "louse," "lousy," and "nit-picking." We use these words all the time without thinking about the image; perhaps a little discussion and trying to see the picture behind the expression can turn these clichés into fresh comparisons for your students.

> **Keep in Mind**
> We have said before that we do not spend much, if any, class time talking about what a metaphor is, or clarifying the distinction between metaphor and simile. We do, however, focus on metaphor as a lens through which we see the world. When we call somebody a nit-picker, we are seeing that person squinting at tiny white dots on hairs, picking at those dots with thumb and forefinger, and cracking those little white dots between fingernails. Intense attention to the trivial—that's nit-picking. Metaphor enriches our vision because it helps us see more and enriches our language.

Writing Poetry

Before beginning your own poem, reread "Water Boatmen" one more time with your class, with everyone performing the rowing. Suggest that together you create another insect poem, again something that can be performed. Look over the list of insect-like expressions that were brainstormed, and ask the students if they want to add more, since you'll be choosing from this list.

37

Have students select one of the insect comparisons for the whole group to build a poem on. Through discussion and physical demonstration, the group can flesh out details of how the insect looks, sounds, feels, and so on. As they talk, you can write what they say on the board (where it is easy to change it as the class revises).

Once there is a draft on the board of what the class wants in the poem, the students can decide on a key word (like Stroke!) that can be repeated enough to establish the major beat. How can that key word be performed? The students and you can try various movements, and decide on one.

Together, then decide how the lines should be arranged. Does your class want to make their poem for two voices? Does the class prefer to make this poem more of a monologue than a dialogue? Where do they want which lines to go? What changes do they want within the lines to sharpen the image or tighten the rhythm? Are they considering the sounds of the phrases?

When the class has created the poem it wants, you can perform it as an entire group, perhaps a couple of times.

As a final, more individual poetry writing activity, have the class break into small groups. Tell each group to pick other insects from the brainstormed list and create their own performance poems, following the steps the entire group has just gone through. Here's an example we played around with, using "nit-picking."

Pick pick pick	pick pick pick
We're nit-pickers	
pick pick pick	pick pick pick
	finding faults
in the smallest thing	
pick pick pick	pick pick pick
we're nit-pickers	we're nit-pickers

Making Connections

Your students may want to record their poems on audio- or video-tape; such recordings make a fine accompaniment to the clean typed copies of their poems that the students place in their poetry folders, which are described in Chapter 1.

For this lesson, you can also encourage those students who have children at home to perform the poems for the kids and even to try writing some at home with the family. The whole family may enjoy creating insect metaphors, for example, from a youngster's assertion that a sibling is a "stink bug" to a daughter's assertion that her mother is a "queen bee." These in turn can be shared with the class.

In this lesson, students learn that new vocabulary is understandable if it is in meaningful context and meaningfully interacted with. Also, strong rhythm in poetry is conducive to oral performance, maybe with table drumming, hand clapping, foot tapping, or other performance back-up. Physical movements can make the poem both more enjoyable and more easily understood.

Summing Up

Chapter 6

MUSIC AS NARRATIVE POETRY

Why Music?

Here, we focus on music as narrative—that is, music that tells a story. Most popular music tells a story in a very limited number of words and contains all the elements of a narrative: themes, plots, conflicts, settings, and characters. Students can explore and learn how stories are put together by hearing, reading, and writing short musical pieces. This lesson provides a bridge between students' everyday life and a particular kind of poetry.

Most people listen to poetry in songs on a regular, if not daily, basis. Whether it is rock-and-roll, country-and-western, rap, easy listening, religious, opera, or folk, music allows us and our students to make connections between poetry as heard in music and written poetry. All the elements of poetry can usually be found in music: oral and aural familiarity, high appeal, rhyme, rhythm, repetition, images, and often strong emotional content.

Good Advice

There are many different kinds of music, and not all of it is appreciated by everyone. Some lyrics and topics might be offensive to some people. Thus, you and your students will have to determine what is appropriate for whole-class, small-group, partner, and individual use. It is vitally important to be direct with the students about this matter. We tell our students that before a particular piece of music is used with the whole class, we and the individual who brings in the piece of music will discuss the lyrics, length, and so on. We stress that this is simply an act of common courtesy to other members of the class.

This is an extended lesson that will take more than one class meeting. First, read the lesson, then read the lyrics and listen several times to the songs you will be using.

We have built this lesson around two songs, one secular and the other sacred: "John Henry" is a popular, traditional song that has been recorded by various folk singers over the years; "Amazing Grace" has been sung in many languages by many different groups and individuals. We think that at least one of these songs will be appropriate for most groups. However, if neither is, then the lesson itself can be easily modified to accommodate other pieces of music.

We include one version of "John Henry" here, but like most folk music, it has different versions. You may be able to find recordings of the song by African American singers in your local library.

John Henry

When John Henry was a little baby boy,
You could hold him in the palm of your hand,
He gave a long and a lonesome cry,
"Gonna be a steel-drivin' man,
  Lawd, Lawd, Gonna be a steel-drivin' man."

Well, the captain said to John Henry,
"Gonna bring that steam drill 'round,
Gonna take that steam drill out on the job,
Gonna whop that steel on down,
  Lawd, Lawd, Gonna whop that steel on down."

John Henry said to the captain,
"Well, a man ain't nothin' but a man,
And before I let a steam drill beat me down,
Gonna die with the hammer in my hand,
  Lawd, Lawd, Gonna die with the hammer in my hand."

They took John Henry to the tunnel,
Put him in the lead to drive,

(continued)

John Henry (continued)

The rock so tall, John Henry so small,
That he laid down his hammer and cried,
  Lawd, Lawd, Laid down his hammer and cried.

John Henry said to his shaker,
"Now, Shaker, why don't you sing?
I'm throwin' nine pounds from my hips on down,
Just listen to the cold steel ring,
  Lawd, Lawd, Just listen to the cold steel ring."

Well, the man that invented the steam drill,
He thought he was mighty fine,
But John Henry drove his fifteen feet,
And the steel drill only made nine,
  Lawd, Lawd, The steam drill only made nine.

John Henry looked up at the mountain,
And his hammer was striking fire,
He hammered so hard that he broke his heart
And he laid down his hammer and he died,
  Lawd, Lawd, He laid down his hammer and he died.

They took John Henry to the tunnel,
And they buried him in the sand,
And ev'ry locomotive comes a-roarin' by
Says, "There lies a steel-drivin' man,
  Lawd, Lawd, There lies a steel-drivin' man."

Here are the lyrics for "Amazing Grace." Again, you may be able to find various recordings of this religious hymn in your local library.

Amazing Grace
by John Newton

Amazing grace, how sweet the sound
that saved a wretch like me.
I once was lost but now am found,
was blind but now I see.

'Twas grace that taught my heart to fear,
and grace my fears relieved;
how precious did that grace appear
the hour I first believed.

The Lord has promised good to me,
his word my hope secures;
he will my shield and portion be
as long as life endures.

Through many dangers, toils, and snares,
I have already come,
'tis grace that brought me safe thus far,
and grace will lead me home.

Starting the Lesson

- Brainstorm with students about the kinds of music they like, listen to, and sing on a regular basis. Where do they listen to it? On the car radio? At home? Work? List the types of music on the chalkboard or newsprint. Be sure to share your own favorites.

- Discuss as a whole class what makes people like a particular kind of music. For example, someone might like religious hymns because of their messages of love and salvation, rap because of its word play, rock-and-roll because of its driving beat, country-and-western because of its frequent wit and humor, and so forth. List these reasons on the board or newsprint next to the other brainstormed list.

- Play for the students either "John Henry" or "Amazing Grace." Then give them the printed lyrics and allow them to read along as you play it a second time.

- After they have listened to it the second time, ask if anyone has heard it before. We're sure that some of your students will be familiar with "John Henry," an American version of the conflict between man and machine. John Henry heroically matched himself against the steam drill and defeated it, but the battle "broke his heart, and he laid down his hammer and he died." It is no wonder that this man's strength, courage, and perseverance made him a folk hero. He is a working man made obsolete by technology. Your students might have their own stories of being displaced by technology or by corporate "downsizing."

- If you play "Amazing Grace," then elicit from students their ideas about the events that led the composer to write the song. You might want to have the students do this in pairs. As a whole group share the different ideas. They all will probably deal with some sort of spiritual crisis. If no one knows the background of the hymn, tell them that it was written by a slave trader in the 1800s who was "saved" by amazing grace during a personal spiritual crisis; he then became an outspoken foe of slavery. You also might want to point out the universal popularity of the hymn. Bill Moyers did a full hour program on public television about "Amazing Grace"; this tape is available at many video rental stores.

- Play the song again and encourage everyone to sing along, perhaps joining in during the last two repeated lines of each verse of "John Henry" or singing the whole of "Amazing Grace." The repetition of the song, together with a discussion of what the story is about (what the song "means") makes the lyrics readable.

Keep in Mind

Both of these pieces are emotional stories. Be sure that you and your students take time to feel the songs and to talk a bit with one another about how the songs make you feel. It is important that we *respond* to the work of art before we start to analyze it.

- After you have sung and responded to the song, explore with students what makes it poetic. Students will probably focus on the rhythm, rhyme, and repetition. Be sure to point out also the figurative language and imagery; for example, John Henry gives a long and lonesome cry as a baby even though you could "hold him in the palm of your hand," and we can hear the "cold steel sing" and see his hammer "striking fire." Look at the way the song uses vernacular language to great effect: we almost can *feel* the steam drill "whop that steel on down." Chances are that you and your students will see that one phrase exemplifies more than one poetic aspect. The repetition of "Lawd, Lawd," for instance, is a refrain signaling that the last line will be repeated, so it helps mark the stanzas; it also intensifies the meaning of the last, repeated line. Using "Lawd, Lawd" this way typifies the kind of rural speech we often think of as "folksy"; the spelling "Lawd" intensifies this folksiness.

In "Amazing Grace" the narrator calls himself a "wretch" who was imprisoned by his sins and freed by god's grace, who was lost and then found. This hymn of thankfulness does not show us the vivid images that "John Henry" does, but the narrator's obvious depth of feeling touches most listeners.

Writing Poetry

To begin writing poetry in this lesson, have students break up into small groups and brainstorm topics that they think might be developed into a song. "John Henry" tells the story of a mythic American figure, while "Amazing Grace" tells a more universal story of spiritual crisis and redemption. If you use "John Henry," students might list events in their own working lives or some of the issues and images that surface from the discussion of the song. Using "Amazing Grace" might result in topics such as brotherly love and world peace.

Encourage the small groups to select one topic and generate ideas, lines, and rhymes that would contribute to a song. Tell them that they can use the pattern of the song you listened to, some other pattern they are familiar with, or one that they make on their own. (Most students will use the pattern of a known song.) Their song does not have to be long. It might only be two or three stanzas.

Instruct each group to have one person act as a recorder. Tell them not to worry about spelling; just write down the song. If you're working with one student or a small class of three to four, then you might serve as the recorder. If tape recorders are available, groups might also tape their discussions and ideas. Circulate and participate with each group. Don't be afraid to offer your ideas, but be careful not to dominate with "teacher talk," directing students and their ideas.

Once students in a group have completed their first attempt of a song, have them sing it among themselves. If they are shy or reticent, be sure to join in with your vocal support. As they sing it, all of you pay attention to the way it flows. Is it easy to sing? Does it rhyme? Does it tell the story the students want to tell? After the group sings it a few times and perhaps makes any changes, ask the students to prepare a final version and copy of the song. This is where spelling, capitalization, punctuation, and computer use come into play. We deal with these in the chapter "What About Skills?"

Once all groups have written songs that they like and have prepared final copies of the lyrics, make enough copies for all the students so at the next meeting the class can have a sing-along. Encourage each group to first sing its song, and then with printed copies of the lyrics have the rest of the class join in for a second singing. This repeated group singing will support the least proficient readers. The sing-along might take a substantial part of a class meeting. You can also preserve these songs in a printed format and on audiotape for future individual and group read- and sing-alongs. This is especially useful for the least proficient readers, who can take the tape and printed lyrics home and listen while they read and sing.

Making Connections

This lesson can be extended in various ways. Encourage students to bring in their favorite music and lyrics. (Remember: tell them that they will share the song with you first before you use it with the whole class.) Use the students' favorites for sing-alongs and as catalysts for additional song writing. Starting or ending each meeting with a song helps build a sense of community and often lifts everyone's spirits. It also gives students repeated practice reading meaningful texts.

The story of John Henry is retold in two fine picture books for children. Ezra Jack Keats's *John Henry: An American Legend* and Julius Lester's *John Henry* could be used in class to spark discussion about the different mental pictures we have of John Henry and how the particular language of the books helps shape those pictures. Also, students who have children might be interested in sharing one or both of the books at home.

There are many collections of traditional songs about working folks, railroads, mining, factories, unions, and the struggles between labor and management. If students are interested, you might bring in one or more of these songs and make connections with "John Henry." For example, Hudie Ledbetter's "Take this Hammer" is a natural complement to "John Henry." You can find this song and others if you dig around in your local library for the collection *Hard Hitting Songs for Hard-Hit People* by Alan Lomax, Woody Guthrie, and Pete Seeger.

This lesson also connects to the one on oral performance and the one on poetry about work. You can draw many comparisons to these lessons.

Summing Up

Poetry reading and writing can be related to the music that your students listen to on a regular basis. Literacy development can be fostered by the reading and writing of these predictable texts—that is, familiar songs that emphasize rhyme, rhythm, repetition, and story. We have learned that the composition and performance of songs encourages literacy as a communal and joyful process.

Chapter 7

POETRY ABOUT WORK

Why Write Poems About Work?

Narrative poetry offers us a chance to explore our own pasts and our own lives. Here, as in the other lessons in this book, the purposes of poetry are to create joy and pleasure and expand our lives. This lesson relates to the previous music lesson, in which you and your students read and write musical poems that tell stories. Most of the activities in this lesson highlight poetry writing by individual students rather than partners or small groups.

This lesson may take two sessions, the first in which your students read and discuss the poem "Waitress" by Alissa Levine, the second in which they write. You and your class may want to expand this topic by reading and writing more about work, so we have included more than one poem at the end of this chapter.

Getting Ready

• Read the lesson, and read aloud the poems a few times. All the poems in this chapter contain the theme of work. Consider which poems your students might enjoy. We use the poem on the next page as a sample.

Waitress

by Alissa Levine

I pick up the phone
and answer to a woman
That yes we are open
until ten at night.

Thank you she doesn't say
"You're welcome."

    Water I bring them
    bread and wine
    They want salad
    I serve it
    and go back to the kitchen
    "Order in" I say
    and give in the bills

    Table four is up
    so's table five
    lasagna
    garlic bread
    Quiche Lorraine
    salmon
    perogies
    fries and gravy

    All served;
    I go 'round with the water
    (we call it watering the cus-
    tomers)

    Back to the kitchen
    my table is up
    two Specials
    done well
    a sour creamed baked potato
    on the side
    They want more wine

    I love to get my customers drunk.

(continued)

Waitress (*continued*)

by Alissa Levine

More wine all 'round
Good.
I hope they notice all the work
I'm doing for them

I expect tips.

At long last they go
or stay and have coffee
and talk and smoke cigarettes

I go 'round to refill
with coffee and cream
A woman passes her
cup to me

Thank you she doesn't say
"You're welcome."

(From *Paperwork: Contemporary Poems from the Job*, edited by Tom Wayman. Copyright 1991 by Harbour Publishing. Reprinted by permission of Alissa Levine.)

- In this lesson, you'll be asking the students to write poems individually, so you'll be moving from one student to another rather than participating in a group creation of a poem. As a model, you will need to write a poem of your own before class meets. To do this, after you have had a chance to reread all the poems we provide a few times, think about your own work and the jobs you've held. Which poem best connects to your life? That's the one you may want to use as a model for your poem about your own work. When you have finished writing your poem, make copies of it and your rough notes, so you can share these with your class.

- Tell your students that you and they will be looking at one or more poems about work and will be writing individual poems about work. Read "Waitress" aloud a couple of times, then show the poem to your students and read it aloud again.

Ask your class to work in pairs or groups of three, reading the poem themselves and telling one another what they think about it.

- After people have had a chance to discuss the poem, the poem should be read aloud again. Perhaps one or two of the students would like to do this, or you can be the reader.

Good Advice

You may get questions about the food names ("lasagna," "perogies," "Quiche Lorraine") in the poem; go ahead and answer these without rereading the poem to get context clues, because that section of the poem does not give you any more hints as to what kind of dishes these are. If any student has worked in a restaurant, that person can answer or explain phrases, such as "hand in the bills," that are peculiar to that job. The expression "watering the customers" is typical of the witty jargon that is particular to each kind of work, from construction to college teaching. You may want to ask what kinds of phrases are special to each student's job and perhaps to list these on the board.

We have used the poem "Waitress" with many different students. They always have spirited discussions about the character of the waitress and about the situation. Good poetry will have multiple interpretations. You and your students do not need to agree on one meaning.

- This is a good time to show the poem you wrote about your work. You can model for the students the process you went through creating the poem, helping them to see how they now can start their poem. Maybe you want to talk about how one of the poems reminded you of your own work and started you jotting words, phrases, and images. Maybe you want to list these notes on the board. Tell the students what you were thinking as you were writing your notes. What questions were you asking yourself? What decisions were you making? Did you wonder whether to make your poem serious or humorous? Did you decide to make it rhyme or not? As you began to select words and phrases, to build the lines and images of your poem, how did you decide where to break a line? We have referred to repetition several times as a device that helps establish the rhythm and musicality of a poem; did you decide to use repetition, and if so, how? What part of your work story did you decide to focus on here? Why? With these insights, you are letting the students see how you approach writing. They need to recognize that no one just dashes off a few stanzas. All poets, beginning and experienced, generate for themselves enough raw material from which they can pick and choose, and can play with.

- After you have talked about the process you followed, give students time to look at your poem, to talk a bit about it, and to ask you questions or make comments. Don't be surprised if someone asks you,

"What does this mean?" and you are embarrassed to discover that you don't quite know. That happens to poets all the time.

- Ask your students if "work" is a topic they are ready to write about. We have had the best results with prompting students to think about their worst job. Students should work in pairs and groups of three as they talk through the poems they are going to write. Perhaps some students are confident enough of themselves as writers to jot some notes. Of course, the poem we talk through before writing will differ from what we actually write. We're not just copying our words to paper.

Keep in Mind

As people write about their lives, sometimes they write about very private and painful events or times. Reliving hurtful experiences can result in powerful poetry, but only the author can decide who should see this poetry. Students may decide not to show you or anyone in class what they've written, and that decision must be respected. Sometimes a student will share with a teacher a poem dealing with intensely painful events; again, only the student can decide who else may read this.

Teachers and tutors are not counselors. Poetry is not therapy. It is possible that a student wants to discuss some experience that you are uncomfortable hearing about. You deserve the same courtesy as you are showing the students: just say, "I am not comfortable talking about this; let's talk about something else."

Writing Poetry

Writing work poems is a way of talking about one's life, but there are other topics that can elicit memories and stories: a first job, first school day, first date, first love, or first heartbreak—all are topics that can call forth personal histories. Asking, "Where were you on the day that a well-known event happened?" also brings up memories. Where were you the day the U.S. space shuttle *Challenger* exploded and took the astronauts and a young school teacher to death below the sea? You probably remember where you were, what you were doing, when you heard the news, and how you felt.

Making Connections

Some good prose references include Studs Terkel's *Working*, a collection of people's descriptions of their jobs, and *The Foxfire Book* and related others edited by Eliot Wigginton, in which people talk about work they do—canning pickles, repairing a chair, and sewing a quilt.

Our own lives are good material for poems. As individual poets, we can use the same processes we used when creating poetry in groups: by talking we generate a list of particulars, select items from that list, and arrange those items as poetically and musically as possible.

Summing Up

Additional Work Poems

These Hips
by Kate Braid

Some hips are made for bearing
children, built like stools
square and easy, right
for the passage of birth.

Others are built like mine.
A child's head might never pass
but load me up with two-by-fours
and watch me
bear.

When the men carry sacks of concrete
they hold them high, like boys.
I bear mine low, like a girl
on small, strong hips
built for the birth
of buildings.

(From *Covering Rough Ground*. Copyright 1991 by Kate Braid. Reprinted by permission of Polestar Press, Ltd.)

Nobody's Heroes
by M.R. Appell

three weeks unemployed

sitting at home

warm & comfortable

when i suddenly

out of the blue

get this job

out on a school roof

wet snow blowing

cold & thick

across the landscape

working with tar

& crushed stone

on a roofing crew

for just above

minimum wage.

come the end

of the day

we ride in the back

of the open truck

through the centre

of town

like battle weary soldiers

but there are no women & children

lining the streets

cheering & waving & throwing kisses

for we are nobody's heroes.

(From *Paperwork: Contemporary Poems from the Job*, edited by Tom Wayman. Copyright 1991 by Harbour Publishing. Reprinted by permission of M.R. Appell.)

Chapter 8

LYRIC POETRY

What Do You Mean, "Lyric"?

Lyric poetry is what many people think of when they hear the word "poetry" or think of "poets." It is typically a very personal form of poetry, an expression of the poet's emotions and insights. Lyric poetry is relatively short (usually no more than a page or two), and it can be rhymed or unrhymed. It also allows for the exploration and expression of personal feelings.

These characteristics make lyric poetry very appropriate for the adult literacy classroom. In many ways it is the easiest poetry for adult literacy students to write: it allows for the expression of any feeling, mood, or idea; it can be written in an open or "free verse" style; and it does not have to be long.

Getting Ready
- Read through the lesson. This lesson will take at least two meetings.
- Read aloud the poems "To Know the Dark" by Wendell Berry and "Acquainted with the Night" by Robert Frost a few times.

To Know the Dark
by Wendell Berry

To go in the dark with a light is to know the light.
To know the dark, go dark. Go without sight,
and find that the dark, too, blooms and sings,
and is traveled by dark feet and dark wings.

—✺—

(From *Farming: A Hand Book.* Copyright 1970 by Wendell Berry. Reprinted by permission of Harcourt Brace & Company.)

Acquainted with the Night

by Robert Frost

I have been one acquainted with the night.
I have walked out in rain—and back in rain.
I have outwalked the furthest city light.

I have looked down the saddest city lane.
I have passed by the watchman on his beat
And dropped my eyes, unwilling to explain.

I have stood still and stopped the sound of feet
When far away an interrupted cry
Came over houses from another street,

But not to call me back or say good-by;
And further still at an unearthly height
One luminary clock against the sky

Proclaimed the time was neither wrong nor right.
I have been one acquainted with the night.

- After reading both poems a few times, look at them more carefully. What are the poets' feelings about going out into the night? What's the mood in each poem? The language in both poems is conversational, the kind that we can hear every day (except for the end rhyme, of course). There is only one obvious metaphor used, and that is in Frost's poem where he refers to the moon as "One luminary clock."

- Think about your experiences of going out into the night. Are they in any way similar to Berry's and Frost's? How? How are they different? Does it make any difference if you go out into the night in the city or country? Does it make any difference if you are male or female? What about going out into the night alone or with one or more friends?

- Now think about one particular experience of going out into the night. Write some words, phrases, ideas, and images that you associate with that experience. After you have a list, arrange some of the items into a short lyric poem. It doesn't have to rhyme. Here are two poems we wrote that capture our experiences with the night. This one is positive and uses end rhyme:

> We had walked the night away.
> Hand in hand we had tried to say
> What was dearest to our hearts,
> And how the other would play a part.

This one deals with a negative experience:

> I saw it before I felt it
> the fist coming at my right temple
> the sprawl backwards on the sidewalk
> the hand in my back pocket
> wallet gone and helpless
> in the neon night

Keep in Mind

As we use poetry to explore our lives and to express our thoughts and feelings, sometimes the explorations are painful and the expressions angry, confused, or sad. Some poems move us to tears; we try to keep ourselves open to poems of rage, grief, and bitterness as well as to those of joy and delight. This lyric poetry lesson revolves around the two night poems by Berry and Frost and the students' own experiences with the night. These can be emotion-charged experiences. Your students might have fallen in love in the nighttime, had visionary experiences under the stars, or remember the haunting song of a coyote or the summer small talk of their parents on a distant August evening. However, they might also remember acts of violence or fearful childhood experiences. If you are uncomfortable, or if you think your students might be uncomfortable with the discussion and poetry that might result from these two night poems, you might focus instead on love using Trevor Mullings's and A.E. Housman's poems. But whatever topic you use with lyric poetry, be prepared for possible strong feelings, talk, and writing.

Starting the Lesson

- Read Wendell Berry's "To Know the Dark" to your students. It is a short poem, so let them hear it at least twice.

- Show the poem to your students and read it a third time. Tell them to read along with you silently or orally if they choose.

- Ask the students to share their thoughts on the poem with a classmate. After a few minutes, ask them to voice their reactions with the whole class. Have they had similar experiences? Have they gone out into the night with a flashlight and seen only the spot of light in front of them? Have they ever been silent in the night and seen and heard the owls, bats, and cats moving about?

- Now read Robert Frost's "Acquainted with the Night." Maybe your students will want to close their eyes, listen, and try to imagine the person in the poem walking about in the night. Hearing a second reading helps that visualization.

- After the second reading, ask small groups of three or four to tell one another what they saw as they listened. Have those who want to share with the whole class do so.

- Read the poem again, this time having the students follow along; tell them that they can read orally with you if they like.

- Ask your students to talk about both poems. How do they react to both? How does each make them feel? Is Frost's poem as upbeat as Berry's? Berry gives us instructions on how to go outside and see the richness of the night; Frost actually takes us into that night.

> ### Please Note
> We are *not* recommending an in-depth analysis, but we do think it is important for your students to see how poets carefully choose words to express themselves. Berry does; Frost does; and your students can. Berry's "To Know the Dark" uses a limited number of everyday words and repeats them: "dark" is used six times, "go" three times. Almost all the words are single syllable. Look at the language and images Frost uses: "rain," "saddest," "dropped my eyes," "unwilling to explain," "an interrupted cry." No wonder some students find this poem serious and sad.

Writing Poetry

Before writing lyric poetry, encourage your students to talk in pairs about a particular experience, feeling, or idea that they have about going out into the night. Remember to note the advice in the box on page 58.

Share with students the poem that you composed about the night. Explain to them how you went about writing it. Then encourage them to write some of the words that they used when they were talking about their night experiences, feelings, and ideas with one another. Tell them not to worry about spelling right now. (See our suggestions in the "What About Skills" section.) For beginning writers, circulate and assist where needed. The language experience approach works well here. Simply have the student dictate his or her poem to you while you write *exactly* what he or she says. Reading and rereading what the student dictates and asking, "Is this what you want me to write?" will allow the beginning writer to concentrate on the poem's creation and not on the mechanics of writing.

Once the students have generated a written list, ask them to take some of the items from the list and arrange and expand them into a short poem. Once they get their poem on paper, they can see if every word contributes to the emotion they want to express. Remind them that Berry and Frost used everyday language to convey the exact mood and message they wanted.

Encourage the students as they are writing to talk and bounce ideas off others. Writing doesn't have to be silent; sometimes we get good ideas from talking to someone while we write. Circulate and assist those students who need additional help. Allow students to work on their poems until the end of the class or for as long as needed.

If students have not completed their poems by the end of the class or want to polish them further, they can do so at home. Ask them to bring back their poems for the next class.

Making Connections

At the next class meeting have those students who want to share their night poems read them aloud. Depending on the size of the class, this might be done in small groups. You want to be sure that all those who want to share are able to do so in an unhurried manner. Be sure to allow time for comments, observations, and appreciation from students.

If the class is interested, they can produce clean and final copies using a typewriter or word processor and photocopy machine. Depending on the facilities available, students can help with the typing, copying, and collating. These poems can then be used as a regular part of the students' reading materials.

This lesson on lyric poetry can be extended almost indefinitely. Using some of the poems at the end of this lesson, students can write about their feelings concerning love, marriage, divorce, war, and other issues.

Summing Up

Lyric poetry allows students to explore and express personal experiences and emotions. In this lesson and in others, pairing poems on a given topic is often a useful way of generating discussion, insight, and writing. And, as mentioned earlier, encouraging students to share, talk, and assist one another while writing often fosters both more writing and a sense of community in a class.

Additional Lyric Poems

We've included a few examples of poems that we enjoy reading aloud and discussing with a friend, relative, or co-worker. These poems might easily be used later as the basis for another lesson.

Here's William Carlos Williams's personal response to the morning star:

"El Hombre" (The Man)

by William Carlos Williams

It's a strange courage

you give me ancient star:

Shine alone in the sunrise

toward which you lend no part!

※

In this next poem, Robert Francis meditates on the language that we often use during war time and on what that language really means:

Light Casualties

by Robert Francis

Light things falling—I think of rain,
Sprinkle of rain, a little shower
And later the even light snow.

Falling and light—white petal-fall
Apple and pear, and then the leaves.
Nothing is lighter than a falling leaf.

Did the guns whisper when they spoke
That day? Did death tiptoe on his business?
And afterwards in another world

Did mourners put on light mourning,
Casual as rain, as snow, as leaves?
Did a few tears fall?

※

Trevor Mullings, an adult literacy student from New York City, expresses his feeling for a young woman he saw only briefly on a bus in his poem "The Image of a Person":

The Image of a Person
by Trevor Mullings

I was going home yesterday
on the bus.

And I saw this girl.
She was so beautiful
that I could not take
my eyes off her.

And when I got home,
it was like a picture
in my mind.

———

(From *From My Imagination*. Copyright 1990 by Trevor Mullings. Reprinted by permission of New Readers Press.)

Linda Pastan takes a much harsher look at love gone bad in her following poem:

Soup

by Linda Pastan

"A rich man's soup—and all from a few
stones." Marcia Brown, *Stone Soup*

If your heart feels
like a stone
make stone soup of it.
Borrow the parsley
from a younger woman's garden.
Dig up a bunch of rigid carrots.
Your own icebox is full
of the homelier vegetables.
Now cry into the pot.
When he comes home
serve him a steaming bowlful.
Then watch him as he bites
into the stone.

(From *PM/AM: New and Selected Poems.* Copyright 1982 by Linda Pastan. Reprinted by permission of W.W. Norton & Company.)

In this poem, Langston Hughes wittily expresses his personal credo:

Motto

by Langston Hughes

I play it cool
And dig all jive—
That's the reason
I stay alive.

My motto,
As I live and learn
Is
Dig and be dug
In return.

(From *The Panther and the Lash* by Langston Hughes. Copyright 1951 by Langston Hughes. Reprinted by permission of Alfred A. Knopf, Inc.)

Chapter 9

FOUND POETRY

What Do You Mean, "Found Poetry"?

Found poetry is exactly what its name implies: it is poetry and interesting uses of language that we find every day in our environment. We stressed in another chapter that people often talk poetically without being aware of it. The closer we listen to people, the more poetic elements we can hear. We hear witty expressions, descriptive slang or jargon, and folk sayings such as, "She's as snug as a bug in a rug" and "He's as stubborn as a blue-nosed mule in the barn." Just listen to the poetry you hear in these headlines from a newspaper as you read them out loud: "Snow Star Ice Cream"; "Assorted Squash: Acorn Butternut Buttercup"; "Dip, Dip, Hooray! Mootown Snackers"; "The Meatless McCartneys: Conversion Occurred as Lambs Gamboled"; "Robinson Sparks Spurs."

Here is an advertisement from a grocery flyer: "Scrumptious, fresh baked breads and pastries, sugar free desserts, tantalizing chocolates, homemade salads, lo-fat cheeses, and a fantastic soup and salad bar." By simply playing around with the arrangement of the words on the page we can produce something that looks and sounds poetic. We'll even give it a title:

At the Deli

Scrumptious
fresh baked breads
pastries
sugar free
desserts
tantalizing
chocolates

homemade
salads
lo-fat cheeses
fantastic
soup and salad
bar

Found poetry also includes serendipitous writing. Sometimes by looking more closely at a note, shopping list, or letter, we discover the poetic elements in it. Here is a well-known poem by William Carlos Williams. It is said to have been originally written as a note he left for his wife:

This Is Just to Say
by William Carlos Williams

I have eaten

the plums

that were in

the icebox

and which

you were probably

saving

for breakfast

Forgive me

they were delicious

so sweet

and so cold

⤙⧓⤚

(From *William Carlos Williams: Collected Poems 1909–1939, Volume I.* Copyright 1938 by New Directions Publishing Corp. Reprinted by permission of New Directions Publishing Corp.)

Williams's rearrangement of the note with his concern for the rhythm, emphasis of particular words, and sound of the last two lines, "so sweet / and so cold," all help to transform his note into a poem.

Found poetry is fun to read and write. More importantly, found poetry encourages adult developing readers and writers to pay closer attention to the print that surrounds them in their daily lives. It fosters students' appreciation of the most common or simple texts, both their own and those written by others. It celebrates the poetry that we all speak and write naturally, if only we take the time to recognize it. Last, found poetry is something that adult students can share and play around with at home. Writing and reading this poetry is an ideal parent-child activity that will help promote intergenerational literacy.

Getting Ready

- Read through the complete lesson.
- At least a few weeks before the lesson collect newspapers with advertisements, grocery flyers, and coupons.
- Gather enough pairs of scissors, tape, markers of different colors, and blank paper for your students' use.
- Read aloud several times "This Is Just to Say." Try reading it as a simple note. Then read it as a poem, emphasizing the rhythm of the lines.
- Write a note poem, a grocery list poem, and a sports metaphor poem, which are all described later in this chapter, as models for your students.

Starting the Lesson

- Write the poem "This Is Just to Say" on the chalkboard or on newsprint without line breaks and with punctuation. Read it aloud to your students while they follow along. Read it a second time.
- Then ask your students if they write notes to other people in their households, notes that they perhaps tape to the refrigerator ("Don't eat all the ice cream!") or leave on the kitchen table or dresser ("Take out the garbage. Then do your homework. I'll be home late. Love, Mom.").
- Encourage a whole-class discussion of the kinds of notes people write, why they're written, and where they're placed.
- Show the class the correct form of "This Is Just to Say." Read it aloud a couple of times, emphasizing the rhythm of the lines. Have the class read it with you as a poem. Then read it together once again as a note. Explore with students what makes one a poem and the other a note. They will probably comment on the arrangement of the words on the page and the attention to particular words through placement; perhaps they'll also note rhythm and repetition.

There are many ways of creating found poetry. We're going to describe three types of poems you can write: note poems, grocery list poems, and sports metaphor poems. You can create one or more with your students, and you can modify and extend the lessons as you and your students become more comfortable with the forms.

Writing Poetry

Note Poems

To create a note poem, brainstorm with the class a simple note in which you instruct someone to do something. Decide as a group on the person and what you want him or her to do. For example, you might want to leave a note for the janitor: "Dear Bob, Please empty the trash can and wash the board." Once you have decided on a note and have written it on the board or chart paper, have the students play around with ways of shaping it into a more poetic form. Here are some samples we have written:

Dear Bob

Please
empty the trash
   can
and wash the
   board

Dear
Bob, Please!
   EMPTY
the trash can
   WASH
the board!

After experimenting as a whole class with turning the note into a poem, have students break into pairs. Instruct them first to write a note to you or someone else in the class with instructions to do something. After they have written the note, tell them to try to arrange it into a note poem. Tell them not to worry about spelling or punctuation. Circulate and offer encouragement and assistance where needed.

Have the students pass their notes and note poems to those for whom they were written. Give the people who received notes time to read them silently and practice reading them aloud, both as notes and as poems. If someone needs assistance with reading a note, you or the author of the note can read the message aloud to the person.

Encourage students who have children to write notes to one another in the form of poetry at home. Have them bring such notes to class if they'd like to share.

Grocery List Poems

For this type of poetry, have your students work in pairs or trios; larger groups become unwieldy. Pass out the newspapers with grocery flyers and coupons. The students will be grateful that you have brought in scissors, tape, and paper for their poems.

Encourage students to go through the newspapers and compose a grocery list poem. Ask them to focus on the sounds of the items; their list poems should be pleasing to the ear. Show them the one you wrote. Here's one that we composed:

Shopping List
Haychia persimmons
Delicious Dancy
Tangerines
Tomatoes and Turkey Breasts
Brown-n-Serve Rolls
Radishes and Round
Roast Boneless

We thought that the easiest way to compose this poem was to group words according to their beginning and middle letter sounds ("Delicious/Dancy," "Rolls/Radishes," and Round/Roast"). This is also a natural, purposeful, and inductive way of creating and thinking about sound-symbol relationships.

If you are able to bring in large sheets of newsprint, students can write their poems with markers and can paste on pictures of the items cut from the newspapers to make a collage. Display and share the poems with the whole class. Encourage your students to talk about how they selected and arranged the words.

As with the other poetry, encourage students who have children to try the same thing at home. This is an easy and fun way for them and their children to read and write together. Suggest that they bring in and share with the class any grocery list poems that they write at home with their children.

Sports Metaphor Poems

One place we regularly find poetic uses of language is in the sports section of the newspaper. Sports writers typically make use of violent metaphors: for example, "Vandals Trim Eagles' Feathers," "Cowboys Lasso Colts," and "Braves Skin Twins." Metaphor is at the heart of poetry. It says that one thing is something else and helps us see that thing differently, as in "My love is a red, red rose" or "Joe is a vulture."

Have students get together in partner or trio teams. Give each team several sports sections from the newspaper, scissors, paper, tape, and markers. They will compose sports poems by combining and possibly adding to metaphors found in the newspapers.

Show them the sports poem you wrote. Here is an example we wrote. We picked three headlines for their metaphors and one—"Buechler Feels Rescued"—for its sounds. These are the headlines: "Lightning Makes Swimmer Bolt"; "Cards Cut Two Players"; and "Celtics Zing Poor-Shooting Suns." We arranged them into the following poem:

> Cards cut two players
> Celtics zing
> Poor-shooting Suns
> Lightning makes swimmers
> Bolt but Buechler feels rescued

After your students see this example, or one that you have created, ask them to start working together to create their own. They can find various metaphors in the sports section, cut them out, add to them if necessary, and then arrange and tape them on paper in a witty or funny manner. They might want to focus not only on the images the metaphors create but also on the sounds of the words and how they are put together. Circulate and give encouragement where needed.

Have students share their completed sports metaphor poems with the rest of the class. Reading by the whole class and discussion of particular words, images, and metaphors will be useful for beginning readers and budding poets.

Making Connections

Ask students to find examples of visual poetry in commercials on television and radio and to share these examples with the whole class. Spend at least a few minutes each class session sharing such finds. Be sure that you bring in at least one example for possible sharing. The class may want to put up a 9" x 12" envelope for collecting such examples, or if you are fortunate enough to have a bulletin board, the class may want to devote one section to weekly examples of found poetry.

This lesson on found poetry can be tied easily to the lesson on humorous poetry in the following chapter.

Summing Up   Found poetry is a viable and lively way of connecting students to the print in their environment.

Chapter 10

HUMOROUS POETRY

What's Funny About Poetry?

As we have emphasized, poetry enables us to explore and better understand our world and ourselves and helps us express our feelings, beliefs, and ideas. Poetry also increases our fun with language. There are many humorous poems that have been written. Some are as short as a line and some as long as a book. These poems can be pure nonsense, sarcastic social and political commentary, or simply witty ways of looking at our world and ourselves. Humorous poetry is one kind of poetry that many of us know, like, and remember from our childhood. Children have giggled over this jump-rope rhyme for generations:

> Cinderella
> dressed in yella
> went upstairs to kiss her fella.
> Made a mistake
> and kissed a snake.
> How many doctors did it take?
> One, two, three, ...

Many adults enjoy the humor of limerick poetry:

> I sat next the duchess at tea.
> 'Twas just as I feared it would be:
> Her rumblings internal
> Were simply infernal.
> And everyone thought it was me.

This lesson connects to several of the others in this handbook, especially to object poetry, form poetry, and found poetry. This lesson is also valuable for those students who have children; after writing a number of funny poems in class, they easily can do the same thing with their children at home.

We have included four humorous poems for you to share with your students, and we will describe a number of ways to write some funny poems. We are suggesting that the whole class walk through an activity and then break into small groups to create more individual poems. We do not expect you to read and write all of these in a single lesson; rather, we want to provide you with some options. Try out one or more with your students, so you and they will discover which ones are the most fun for you.

Getting Ready

- Read through the complete chapter. We've included enough material here for several lessons.

- Choose the poems that you want to use with your students. We have included the following four poems, but you may have a favorite funny poem of your own:

  "Song Against Broccoli" by Roy Blount, Jr.

  "The Sea-Gull" by Ogden Nash

  "Epitaph on a Waiter" by David McCord

  "Phizzog" by Carl Sandburg

- Read aloud the poems a number of times, enjoying the sound play that contributes to the humor of the poems.

Song Against Broccoli
by Roy Blount, Jr.

The neighborhood stores are all out of broccoli,
Loccoli.

—⌁⌁⌁—

(From *One Fell Soup or I'm Just a Bug on the Windshield of Life* by Roy Blount, Jr. Copyright 1982 by Roy Blount, Jr. Reprinted by permission of Little, Brown & Company.)

The Sea-Gull

by Ogden Nash

Hark to the whimper of the sea-gull;

He weeps because he's not an ea-gull.

Suppose you were, you silly sea-gull,

Could you explain it to your she-gull?

——◦◦◦——

Epitaph on a Waiter

by David McCord

By and by

God caught his eye.

——◦◦◦——

Phizzog
by Carl Sandburg

This face you got,
This here phizzog you carry around,
You never picked it out for yourself,
      at all, at all—did you?
This here phizzog—somebody handed it
      to you—am I right?
Somebody said, "Here's yours, now go see
      what you can do with it."
Somebody slipped it to you and it was like
      a package marked:
"No goods exchanged after being taken away"—
This face you got.

(From *Good Morning, America* by Carl Sandburg. Copyright 1928 and renewed 1956 by Carl Sandburg. Reprinted by permission of Harcourt Brace & Company.)

Starting the Lesson

- Play around with writing some funny poems. Try your hand at the funny comparison, metaphor, situation, and description poetry described later in this chapter.

- Begin by telling your students a few knock-knock jokes. There are many collections of knock-knock jokes available at your library and bookstore, or you might want to ask children for some knock-knock jokes; they usually know several. For example, try the following:

Knock, knock.	Who's there?
Butcher.	Butcher who?
Butcher feet on the floor.	
Knock, knock.	Who's there?
Banana.	Banana who?
Knock, knock.	Who's there?
Banana.	Banana who?
Knock, knock.	Who's there?
Orange.	Orange who?
Orange you glad I didn't say banana again?	

- Ask your students to share some knock-knock jokes that they know.

- After exchanging knock-knock jokes, explore with students how and why they are funny. Usually it is because two words sound the same or almost the same; this is the basis of puns and much humor. Poets such as Ogden Nash stretch this sort of similarity, as he did in "sea-gull, ea-gull, she-gull." As speakers of English, or any other language, we have a *natural* ability to play with the sounds of our language. Babies do it when they babble "ma-ma-ma-ma"; we do it with puns, daily speech, and daily print.

- Read the poems "Song Against Broccoli" and "The Sea-Gull" aloud once or twice. Have the students read along with you.

- Discuss how these two poems use the same kind of sound play as the knock-knock jokes but also are witty in their comments about broccoli and sea-gulls.

- Read the poem "Epitaph on a Waiter" aloud a couple of times.

- Have students share with a partner their responses to this poem.

Writing Poetry

There are various ways of composing humorous poetry, which we will present. You can focus on a particular type during a lesson and then connect it to another type in a subsequent lesson. These different kinds of humorous poetry are not arranged in any sequence. Jump in and try the ones you and your students enjoy!

Funny Comparison Poems

One way of writing funny poetry is to make outlandish, witty, or ludicrous comparisons, using "as" or "like": for example, "His cooking is as appetizing as a week-old omelet" or "Her new shoes look like they escaped from the zoo." These funny comparisons can be made more poetic by also focusing on the way they sound, as in "His cooking is as appetizing as a plate of peas, poi, and passion fruit."

As a whole class, brainstorm some more lines for either "His cooking" or "Her shoes." Try to make the comparisons ridiculous. After the class has come up with some funny and perhaps fantastic comparisons, ask the students to rephrase some, focusing on the sounds to make the comparisons funnier and more poetic. Then ask the students to shape the poem by selecting some of these comparisons. They can dictate these comparisons to you for writing on the board or newsprint. Here's an example using "His cooking":

His cooking is as appetizing as
a plate of peas, poi, and passion fruit
a bowl of boiled birds and bees
a frying pan full of armadillo fat

Once you and your students have exhausted your ideas on this poem, read the whole thing together. Give it a title.

Now brainstorm with students some possible things or people that might be used as the basis for a humorous comparison poem. Local, state, or national politicians, local buildings or structures that are considered eyesores, or the athletic ability of different sports figures are all possibilities. List the ideas on the board or large sheets of paper.

Once all the students have generated a list, they can work together in small groups of three to four and write a funny comparison poem about one of the topics or any other topic that they might select. Ask them to focus on outlandish comparisons and to pay special attention to the way the words sound together. Remind the students not to worry about spelling, handwriting, or punctuation with this first draft. (The section "What About Skills?" contains suggestions on how to deal with these skills.) Circulate and offer encouragement where needed. The humorous poems will be shared with the rest of the class.

When the groups have completed a first version of their poems, ask your students to share them with the rest of the class. Have each group first practice reading the poem together, and then have them chorally read it to the whole class. Add your voice where needed for support.

If your students want to save these funny comparison poems, they can help make clean copies on a typewriter or word processor. With these final versions, you can help them spell words correctly.

Funny Metaphor Poems

The funny comparison poems are similes using "as" and "like." Funny metaphor poems don't *compare* two things; instead, they assert that one thing *is* something else, as in "Broccoli is a hideout for green worms" and "Broccoli is an unwanted relative of cabbage." Metaphors tend to have more force than similes. Metaphors used in funny, witty, and outlandish ways can make good humorous poetry.

As a whole class, brainstorm funny metaphors to describe Nash's "whimpering sea-gull." What does it do? How does it look, sound, and smell? The focus is on images here. Our list looks like the following.

The sea-gull is
a squawking neighbor
a nosey relative
a flying outhouse
an accurate bomber

If your students are hesitant at first, be prepared to offer some lines to start.

Read aloud the poem as your students develop it with weird and silly metaphors. Help students group the metaphors that seem to work together; for example, the "flying outhouse" and "accurate bomber" lines in our list. The more outrageous the metaphors become, the more fun your class will have with this poetry.

Once you and your students have created a funny metaphor poem, give it a title, and read it together a couple of times.

As another activity, brainstorm with students some possible things that might be used as the basis for a humorous metaphor poem such as famous people, pesky creatures from the outdoors, or familiar objects from around the house. You can write funny metaphor poems about anything.

For the rest of the lesson follow the same format described in the funny comparison poetry activity: small groups create their own metaphor poems then share these with the rest of the class. As with all the poems, these can be copied for the class, as a collection or as contributions to the bulletin board.

Funny Situation Poems

Read aloud "Epitaph on a Waiter." Have partners share their responses to the poem. What, if anything, makes it funny? Discuss as a class the underlying basis of humor in the poem: the poet takes a common experience—waiting impatiently in a restaurant—and cleverly presents that situation in a new light and a witty manner. The poet not only helps us see in a refreshing way but also ties the two lines tightly together by using end rhyme.

Ask students to try writing another funny two-line poem with rhyme. As an example, discuss the situation of waiting in line for the gas pump while the person whose car is blocking the pump is inside buying snacks. Brainstorm the specifics of the situation: How do you feel? What is the other person doing? How slow is the person? Why do you need gas immediately? List all these ideas on the board, and from them have students as a whole class put together the two-line, rhyming poem. If your class generates enough ideas, they can write two or three poems. Here are a couple of examples we wrote:

> If he doesn't leave the restroom fast,
> I am going to run right out of gas.

> I am hot and tired and ready to drop
> And she can't decide on a flavor of pop.

Now brainstorm with students some other possible waiting situations that might be used as the basis for a funny two-line, rhyming poem: standing in line at the supermarket, waiting to get into a movie theater, waiting to place your order in a crowded fast-food restaurant, or waiting your turn in the bathroom. The students might want to think of some other topics instead of waiting.

For the rest of this lesson, follow the same format described in the funny comparison poetry section.

Funny Description Poems

Read Carl Sandburg's "Phizzog" to your students. Share the poem with them and read it again while encouraging them to follow along. You and your students can discuss why Sandburg calls a "face" a "phizzog." Now read the poem aloud together. Ask students to share their thoughts on the poem in small groups of three or four. What do they like about it? Do they think it is funny or clever? Why?

Encourage a class discussion of the poem. Allow the different groups to express their ideas. The poem is witty to us because of the way Sandburg describes the way we acquire our looks: somebody simply gives them to us as a wrapped, unknown package. We have no opportunity to shop around or select what we get. Sandburg plays with sound ("phizzog"/"face"), repetition ("This face you got"/"This here phizzog"/"at all, at all"), and use of vernacular English ("Here's yours, now go see what you can do with it"/"This here"/"This face you got").

After exploring the poem, write as a class a similar witty or funny description poem of some human feature, such as nose, hair, hands, feet, arms, or legs. This kind of humorous poem is more sophisticated than the three previously described—funny comparison poem, funny metaphor poem, funny or witty situation poem—so it might be more difficult to write. We encourage it to be done as a whole-class activity so that everyone can benefit from the ideas and inspirations of others. Brainstorm a list of possible topics and as a class select one.

Have students in pairs talk about some possible ways of describing the human feature and discussing how it was acquired. Encourage them to write their brainstormed ideas if they choose. Circulate and offer encouragement.

After five or ten minutes of partner brainstorming, have students tell their ideas to the class. List them on the board or a large piece of paper. Try to get students to group the ideas in some way, for example, by how the feature is described or how it was acquired.

Now with the brainstormed list ask students to think about how it might be put together as a funny or witty description poem. As the students dictate, read aloud as you write their lines on the board. Your laughter will encourage them to take risks and make wild and silly imaginative leaps. This poem making should be fun! Here is a funny description poem we wrote that uses Sandburg's sound, repetition, and vernacular:

> Those feet you walk on,
> Those dainty feet you float around on,
> Did you find them in a shoe store?
> Those dainty feet—you got them
>   at a mall—ain't I right?
> A clerk at K-Mart grabbed you and said,
>   "Take them! They're the Blue Light Special!"
> There are no returns on Blue Light Specials,
> So you're stuck with those feet you float around on,
> Those feet you walk on.

Once you get a draft of the poem that the class likes, read it together. Tell your students to listen to the sounds of the poem. Are there any word changes that might make it sound better? What about repetition? Can any words or lines be repeated to good effect? Does the poem include some everyday speech? Does the speech sound the way people actually talk? Consider our example of "ain't I right?" Is it a funny, witty, or clever poem? Are there any changes that might make it more so?

Take the final draft home and make a clean copy on a typewriter or word processor. Bring back copies for all the students.

There are numerous sources of funny poetry. You may want some suggestions from your local librarian to use in future lessons. Because much funny poetry is written for children, your students may also enjoy sharing these with their children or grandchildren.

Making Connections

Funny poetry uses all the different features of poetry. It adds extravagance, and it plays with sounds to create humor. All these humorous types can be written many times. They are fun and easy to play around with as a class, as a small group, or individually. These humorous poems, especially the first three, also lend themselves to parent-child writing activities.

Summing Up

Chapter 11

WHAT ABOUT SKILLS?

For many years we have studied, researched, and written about adult literacy, and we have worked with adult literacy students. Whether they are reading or writing, most of our students have been quite concerned about "getting it right." Even when we try to persuade them to relax a little, to focus on meaning and not worry about individual words, much less about individual letters, these students remain concerned about correctness. If they are reading, they want to know exactly what that new word is, and it is hard for them to accept our advice, "Guess and go on" or "Just skip it and go on." If they are writing, they want to know exactly how to spell each word and how to capitalize and punctuate correctly. They often worry that their grammar is not correct.

Our study, research, and work with these students have convinced us that this over-attention to tiny fragments of language and this over-concern with correctness holds these students back. We have all heard the expression, "He can't see the forest for the trees." The students we have worked with often could not see a tree for the leaves. Our students believe there is only one correct way to read or write, and they fear they are not correct. That fear keeps them from taking risks and from making guesses at new words when they're reading and at spellings when they're writing. That fear, that over-concern with correctness, gives them tunnel vision. If you roll up a piece of paper into a tube and look through it at this page, you'll see what we mean by "tunnel vision." Tunnel vision prevents you from seeing enough to build some meaning because it lets you see only individual words or letters or punctuation.

How can we address the very real concerns with correctness our students have and, at the same time, help them relax so that this concern no longer impairs their literacy progress? In this chapter, we suggest general strategies that help our students deal with their concern for correctness, as they learn to pay more attention to meaning and begin to take some small risks. And we outline specific strategies to assist students with phonics, spelling, capitalization, punctuation, and grammar.

General Strategies

Throughout this volume, we have discussed various strategies for you to use to build confidence and collaboration among your students. Here is a summary:

- model for students by oral reading
- use material that encourages prediction
- foster a sense of community within the class
- value individual interpretation
- provide various kinds of structure for students' writing
- use the students' backgrounds and experiences
- support and guide students' risk taking
- participate in all the reading and writing activities

We have found that all these basic strategies help adult students expand their reading and writing abilities. At the same time, they foster an equal and collaborative relationship between the teacher and students and among the students themselves. These strategies affirm that regardless of our literacy abilities, we are all learners together and all have something important to contribute to each lesson. We have also found that students working in a group, rather than isolated with a tutor, quickly lose some of that over-concern with correctness. When a group of people talk about their writing, share it, and support one another, everyone can see that there is no one right way to say or write anything. When an adult has only one other person to share with, and that person tends to correct, the new writer is less likely to relax.

Specific Strategies for Skills

Vocabulary

Students ask different questions about what they are reading: sometimes they want a word read aloud; sometimes they want a word defined; sometimes they are just looking for some support. Our usual response is to refer back to the text.

If a student points and asks, "What's that word?" we reply, "Let me read that section to you," and we read a line or two aloud of the word's context. This is a subtle way to indicate that we believe the student can read without asking someone else to intervene every time he or she finds a new word.

If a student asks, "What does that mean?" we usually say, "Let's see," and we read a line or two aloud. Again, we want to demonstrate that words and phrases get their meanings from their contexts. Many of our students have been taught to look up unfamiliar vocabulary in a dictionary, and although using a dictionary is a good skill, we try to persuade our students that with their own knowledge of the world, plus careful attention to the text itself, they can probably figure out what something means. Most of the time dictionaries or teachers with all the answers are not necessary.

Phonics

Phonics is the systematic relationship of the sound system to the writing system. Learning to read involves learning to associate the sound system with the writing system; however, it involves much more than that. Most of the adult students with whom we have worked have had years of phonics instruction in elementary and secondary school, and they still are not proficient readers. Many of them have not been successful precisely because of an undue attention on phonics. We believe that it is important to focus on phonics indirectly. We want to emphasize meaning and understanding first and then to look at the ways that letters and sounds relate to one another.

We have stressed throughout the lessons in this book the importance of having students hear the poems. Sound is an important part of poetry, and poets use it in various ways for different effects. Let's look at Robert Frost's "Nothing Gold Can Stay" and discuss how we might help students explore the ways Frost uses sound.

Nothing Gold Can Stay

by Robert Frost

Nature's first green is gold,
Her hardest hue to hold.
Her early leaf's a flower;
But only so an hour.
Then leaf subsides to leaf.
So Eden sank to grief,
So dawn goes down to day.
Nothing gold can stay.

(From *The Poetry of Robert Frost*, edited by Edward Connery Lathem. Copyright 1936, 1951, 1956 by Robert Frost. Copyright 1964 by Lesley Frost Ballantine. Copyright 1969 by Henry Holt & Co., Inc. Reprinted by permission of Henry Holt & Co., Inc.)

This poem usually generates very personal responses. We are all aging, and the innocence and expectations of childhood are difficult to hold. After reading the poem aloud several times, you and the class discuss how it relates personally, and then look at the sounds of Frost's poem.

Frost uses end rhyme: "gold/hold," "flower/hour," "leaf/grief," "day/stay." You can help students identify this end rhyme and also other uses of sound. Say aloud "green" and "gold" in the first line, and listen to the initial sound of both words. Do the same with the second line, "Her hardest hue to hold," and with "subsides/sank" and "dawn/down/day." This repetition of sounds helps create the music of this poem. Exploring this repetition can help students better understand the relationships between letters and sounds. The important thing is that you and your students explore these relationships in a complete poem; you are not teaching phonics as an isolated skill.

This kind of indirect attention to phonics will help your students develop a better understanding of letter-sound relationships. By encouraging students to pay attention to sound in their own poems, you can further this understanding. For example, you might have your students think about "soft" sounds, such as *silken slivers of sunlight sifted slowly*, or "loud" sounds, such as *big bawling brat*. Most adults have some experience with this kind of language play. Spend a little time talking about tongue twisters, such as "Peter Piper picked a peck of pickled peppers" or the advertisements, jingles, commercials, and signs we hear and see daily, such as Pete's Pizza Place. Look at the nonsense sounds that are regularly used in comic books and cartoons to represent action: "Scraaaaak! Scrunch! Skarm! Spraat!" Funny poems can be constructed simply by looking through comic books and cartoons, listing all the nonsense words, and then arranging them in a poetic fashion. All these language play activities will give your students a better understanding of phonics than workbook activities ever will.

Spelling

Closely related to phonics is spelling, another concern of many adult students. They are firmly convinced that if they cannot spell everything correctly, they will not be able to read or write proficiently either. The advice we offer in this section is grounded in a great deal of research, and the specific activities we describe we have used with a wide range of students in many different situations.

English spelling is difficult: we can use the same spelling to indicate the same sounds (for example, gold/hold or day/stay), but we can also use different spellings for the same sounds (flower/hour or leaf/grief). We are certainly not suggesting that you spend any time presenting spelling rules about -eaf/-ief or -ower/-our. The spelling rules we heard in school lead writers astray more often than they help: for example, look at -our and -ief, and recall "When two vowels go walking, the first one does the talking." Or remember "I before E except after C," and look at odd words like "neighbor" and "weigh." Instead of rules, we just want our students to appreciate the rhymes and recognize that different letter patterns can result in similar sounds. A rhyme scheme often makes it easier to guess what an unknown word might be.

Spelling serves one primary purpose—writing. You do not have to be a good speller to read (think about all the words you can read but can't spell), and you don't have to be a good speller to write a first or second draft of something. Spelling only becomes important when you want to impress the person who reads what you've written. Think about all of the first drafts you write every day. When we write a shopping list we don't run to a dictionary to see if we have spelled "spageti" correctly. And we don't check our spelling when we leave a note taped to the refrigerator door: "Take out garbidge!" or "Don't eat the leftover enchaladas! There for dinner." Or think of the letters you write to a very close friend. You are less concerned with spelling in those letters than in the business letters you write to strangers. The reason you are writing—the *purpose*—and the person(s) you are writing to—the *audience*—determine the relative importance of spelling. The same applies to punctuation and capitalization.

Spelling serves writing. That is the attitude we want to help our students acquire. If they pay undue attention to spelling, then spelling will certainly interfere with their writing and, ultimately, with their self-confidence as developing readers and writers. Encourage your students to think of spelling as a tool that they should use at appropriate times, not all the time. You can best do this by modeling and suggesting a number of different strategies. Let's look at some that we have found useful.

Strategy 1: Experiment

Spelling (and an understanding of phonics discussed earlier) is developed by experimenting with the letters and sound of the language. The more you can encourage risk taking and language play among your students the better. When your students are writing the first draft of a poem, you want them to concentrate on creating the poem. The words, images, sounds, and rhythm are important. As they are composing the poem, tell them to spell the words the best they can. Tell them that it is important to stay with the ideas and images in the poem they are creating and not to let spelling get in their way. So if the first two lines of a poem in progress are "Four ravens leap / From the canyon rim" and they are unsure about the spelling of "ravens" and "canyon," they might write, "Four ravins leap / From the canyun rim." If they are less sure of the spelling, they might write, "Four rvns leap / From the canyn rim." If they are even less sure, they can simply write the letter they think the word begins with or leave a blank space like this: "4 r———— leap/From the ———— rim."

Strategy 2: Collaborative Editing

Most adult students will want to know when they will fix these misspellings, and it is important to provide different opportunities and strategies for doing so. The best way of fixing the spelling, punctuation, and capitalization on a final draft is to have students edit their poems with a partner, in small groups, or with you. Before going to an editor, a writer needs to look carefully at the piece: Which words does the writer suspect are misspelled? They can be marked. Which sections does the writer feel especially proud of? They can be checked against the editor's perceptions. Is there a section the writer is worried about? That too needs to be brought before the editor.

This kind of social effort not only gets students to think, talk, and share their knowledge of spelling, but it also fosters the kind of collaborative learning that we have stressed throughout this book. Partners and small groups can look closely at the poem for spelling mistakes, discuss alternatives to the way a word is spelled, and finally verify the correct spelling in another poem, text, or dictionary. Resources include dictionaries, handbooks of commonly misspelled words, and hand-held spelling checkers. If your students are composing on the computer and the program has a spelling checker, then this is another tool. Remind your students that these resources are commonly used because most people cannot spell all words.

Strategy 3: Individual Spelling Folders

The more often your students use words in their own writing, encounter the words again and again in their reading, and engage in editing activities, the more likely are they to learn how to spell the words correctly. However, some students still like a more systematic approach. For them, we recommend a spelling folder. This is a file folder or notebook with a line drawn down the center of each page. At the head of one column is "My Guess," and at the head of the other column is "Dictionary Spelling." Under My Guess students list those words that they were unsure of in early drafts. Once they verify their own guesses, or discover the correct spelling through the various editing activities just described, they enter the correct spelling under Dictionary Spelling. It looks like this:

My Guess	Dictionary Spelling
rvns	ravens
canyun	canyon

The students can then use their personal dictionary as a future reference and as a study aid to focus on those particular words that they really want to spell correctly. The spelling folder is especially useful because it encourages students to take risks, but at the same time assures them that they will also learn the correct spelling of words.

Strategy 4: Mini-Lessons

To help students with skills, you can conduct mini-lessons on spelling, capitalization, and punctuation. We call these mini-lessons because they should be brief and to the point and should not take more than 10 or 15 minutes. Spelling, capitalization, and punctuation are tools that help your students create lively and lovely poems. The time spent on these tools should be dramatically less than the time spent on reading and writing poetry. Your mini-lessons should be based on the students' actual writing and needs. We are *not* suggesting that you use commercial programs or worksheets or anything that is unrelated to your students' actual writing.

If you see your students constantly misspelling certain words, you might want to conduct a mini-lesson on those words. Many people misspell "they're" and "their." Some people substitute "there"; some move the apostrophe in the first word; some reverse the vowels in the second. Traditionally, teachers have taught all three words at once, with the injunction: "Don't confuse these!" And of course teaching them all together guarantees confusion. With easily confused words, teach only one at a time; when the students have got that one, then teach the other(s).

Another possible mini-lesson involves the students' individual spelling folders. Ask a student who is quite concerned about spelling to compare the two columns of words, counting one point for every letter that occurs in both My Guess and Dictionary Spelling columns and another point for every letter in order. For example, "thier" and "their " have all five correct letters and have three of five in order. This mini-lesson helps students see what they are doing right.

A third possible mini-lesson is sharing with students the two most commonly used strategies of good spellers. The first is to write possible alternatives for a word, then select the one that looks right. The second is to identify those words that you can never be sure of, and put a list of those handy to the typewriter or word processor. For example, one of us constantly misspells "occurence (occurrence?)" and "questionnaire (questionairre?)" and so makes sure to check each one (using the computer's spelling checker) before publishing.

Punctuation and Capitalization

Because poets use a wide variety of punctuation and capitalization in their work, poetry also offers wonderful opportunities for mini-lessons. Take, for example, the untitled poem by Lucille Clifton on the next page.

Together you and your students can explore where you might use capital letters, commas, and periods. In these mini-lessons you want to get your students to take risks and to articulate why they think a particular word needs to be capitalized or a punctuation mark might be-

Untitled

by Lucille Clifton

listen children

keep this in the place

you have for keeping

always

keep it all ways

we have never hated black

listen

we have been ashamed

hopeless   tired   mad

but always

all ways

we loved us

we have always loved each other

children   all ways

pass it on

long in a certain place. We want our students to see that in English there are usually options; recognizing this helps decrease that over-concern with correctness. The first three lines of Clifton's poem could be written like this: "Listen children,/ keep this in the place / you have for keeping"; or like this: "Listen children, / Keep this in the place / You have for keeping"; or like this: "Listen children! / Keep this in the place / You have for keeping!" Discussion about which of these best captures the tone and mood of the poem will help students further appreciate the poem. It will also make them more aware of the ways we can use punctuation and capitalization. Similar play and exploration in their own writing will continue to develop this awareness.

Grammar

We said earlier that many of our students are concerned about their grammar. What should we do about it? First we have to recognize that, just as there is no single correct way to punctuate or capitalize, there is no single correct way to say anything. More, the heart of poetry is expressing one's self; clearly, there can never be one way to do that. The particular style of speech that each of us has is our voice. Adults who come for help with basic reading and writing are, in an important sense, silent; their voices are not heard. One of our major goals as adult literacy teachers is to help those adults find and use their voices. Poetry offers our students examples of many ways to say things.

Summing Up

- Get it on paper first; fiddle with it second.
- There is no single correct way to spell, punctuate, capitalize, or use grammar.
- Playing with language teaches students better than practicing rules or going through drills.

Chapter 12

PUBLISHING STUDENT WORK

Why?

We think it is important that your students see their work published—neatly typed, copied, and assembled into a book of collected works. When students see that you have typed their work, they know you value that work. For adults in literacy programs, this may be the first time in their lives that someone has cared enough about what they write to type it. When you photocopy student poems and distribute them in class, you are treating student writing the same way you treat commercially published poems by recognized authors. The underlying message—your work is as important as theirs—is clear. Also, having those copies in class allows all the students to reread their own and others' poems, and this rereading makes those poems more predictable and easier to read. You may have found it difficult to obtain material that is adult, relevant, and yet readable; your students' own writing is just such material.

Your students need to see their writing being read by people not in the classroom. Adult new readers and writers often have low opinions of their own abilities. Creating poetry helps students begin to see themselves as competent readers and writers. However, after some time the students may say: "My stuff is okay for guys like me who can't really read or write, but it's not good enough for anyone else to read." They need to see their writing being read by a wider public than their classmates and you.

How?

How do you go about publishing student work? How do you make it available to a wider audience? Let's go through the process step by step.

Audience

Who will be the audience? Sometimes a poem is written only for one's self; in that case you may not even see it, and the author has effectively published it by writing it. It is important to respect an individual's right not to share what he or she has written. Sometimes the act of writing allows us to relive personal experiences that we want to remain private. You as the teacher need to be sensitive to these possibilities and protect your students from potentially embarrassing exposure.

We anticipate that most of the poems generated by your students will be shared. Collections of these poems can be published by being typed, photocopied, and passed out to the class, and copies can kept in a manila folder titled "Our Poems."

We hope your students will publish some poems for readers outside the class. These readers may be their family members, close friends, church members, readers of a shop newsletter, or the general public. The audience determines the type of publication. A poem written to a family member perhaps is best published by being carefully hand lettered on fine paper and maybe rolled and tied with a ribbon. If someone writes a birthday or anniversary greeting, that too can be hand lettered. Someone interested in calligraphy might volunteer to do the lettering. There are computer programs that will print the paper so that it can be folded into a standard greeting card shape. A humorous poem written to a few friends might have a drawing or piece of clip art pasted on, which can then be photocopied. A collection of class poetry that is made available to the general public needs some sort of binding and information about the authors.

Editing

Everybody gets edited. All published writing, whether it be in a newspaper, magazine, book, academic journal article, or business advertisement, is closely edited by someone. You want to stress this to your students. Writers do not want to be embarrassed by mistakes in their work; that's why they value good editors.

Do not take student writing home to mark or correct, only to read and type. It is vitally important that editing be done with the student. You and the author sit together and go over the piece. Be careful about writing on student work; throw away your red pen.

Preparing Final Copy

Students need to do as much of the work as possible: typing on typewriter or computer, selecting or creating illustrations, photocopying, assembling, and binding. If you or they are able to use a computer, the spelling checker can spot misspellings and suggest correct spellings. If a collection of works is being published, the class needs to design the cover, title page, table of contents, and the sort of information about the authors that we generally find on book jackets. Be sure to have the students select the works, illustrations, and format so it is truly their book. It will not mean nearly as much to them if you do all the work and make all the decisions. If any of the students are taking courses in desktop publishing, they can be the class experts on using the computer to prepare and produce the final copy.

For covers, many photocopy firms have cardstock—a thin cardboard—in a wide variety of colors and can photocopy black and white art and lettering onto that cardstock. The same businesses will also bind your collection (with covers) for a small fee.

Submitting to Other Publishers

There are now several publications that feature the writing of adult new writers, and your students certainly should have access to these. They can read what other students are writing, and they can submit their own work. The best known of these is *Voices: New Writers for New Readers*, published by the Lower Mainland Society for Literacy Education in Surrey, British Columbia. Another source for publishing student work is *New Writers' Voices*, published by Literacy Volunteers of New York City. East End Literacy Press in Toronto, Ontario, publishes The New Start Reading Series, which includes such student autobiographies as *My Name Is Rose*. New Readers' Press, the publishing arm of Laubach Literacy International in Syracuse, New York, also publishes student work. Many adult programs publish their own students' work but do not invite submissions from elsewhere. We recommend getting as many of these collections as possible into the class library: your students can read what others have written, can see how their own work compares, and can sense themselves as a part of that growing body called "authors."

Celebrating

Students need to have their new accomplishments in literacy celebrated. When students' writing is published, you and they can make an occasion of it. Certainly when the copies of the class-made books are first passed out, students will read their own pieces and then the pieces of classmates. This quiet celebration can be followed by an author signing, which can range from the informal passing of copies to classmates for them to sign their names to their poems, to a more formal "Meet the Author" occasion, to which family, other classes, and school officials are invited. The school officials should receive copies of the class-made book, and they can ask individual authors to sign their copies. A call to your local newspaper and TV station about the event may result in welcome publicity. Many local newspapers regularly publish poetry by readers, and your students' work might result in a special feature. Perhaps your local library would welcome the class book on its shelves; if you find out that this is so, you may be able to arrange for a formal presentation of the book to the library, again with as much publicity as possible.

RESOURCES

Paperbacks Full of Poems

Collom, J., & Noethe, S. (1994). *Poetry everywhere: Teaching poetry writing in school and in the community.* New York: Teachers & Writers Collaborative.

    Collom and Noethe have created an excellent, inexpensive resource, with clear advice on how to get writing from people of different ages and many examples of their poems.

Dunning, S., & Stafford, W. (1992). *Getting the knack: 20 poetry writing exercises.* Urbana, IL: National Council of Teachers of English.

    Although written for teachers of secondary students, this manual by two well-known poets will make an excellent companion to this handbook.

Gensler, K., & Nyhart, N. (Eds.). (1978). *The poetry connection: An anthology of contemporary poems with ideas to stimulate children's writing.* New York: Teachers & Writers Collaborative.

Koch, K. (1970). *Wishes, lies, and dreams: Teaching children how to write poetry.* New York: Random House.

Koch, K. (1973). *Rose, where did you get that red? Teaching great poetry to children.* New York: Random House.

Koch, K. (1977). *I never told anybody: Teaching poetry in a nursing home.* New York: Random House.

    Koch's three books are available in libraries and second-hand bookshops, and they all contain good advice for new teachers and new writers of poetry.

Padgett, R. (Ed.). (1987). *Handbook of poetic forms.* New York: Teachers & Writers Collaborative.

    This is a good reference work.

E S O U R C E S

Sears, P. (1990). *Gonna bake me a rainbow poem: A student guide to writing poetry*. New York: Scholastic.

Although this book is addressed to students in grades 7 to 12, the many ideas and activities are equally viable for adult readers and writers.

Paperback Anthologies of Poetry About Work

These are extremely suitable for adults. *Paperwork* has the biggest collection; we recommend it highly.

Coles, N., & Oresick, P. (Eds.). (1994). *For a living: The poetry of work*. Champaign, IL: University of Illinois Press.

This is a companion volume to *Working Classics*. The poems explore the nature and culture of nonindustrial work, from mopping floors to dealing on Wall Street. All the poems were written in the 1980s and 1990s.

Downie, G., & Tranfield, P. (Eds.). (1991). *More than our jobs: An anthology*. Vancouver, BC: Pulp Press.

Landale, Z. (Ed.). (1985). *Shop talk: An anthology*. Vancouver, BC: Pulp Press.

Levine, P. (1991). *What work is*. New York: Knopf.

This is a National Book Award winner.

Literacy Volunteers of New York City. (1992). *Speaking out on work: An anthology by new writers*. Literacy Volunteers of New York City.

This brief collection of poetry and prose by adult new writers offers fine examples for other literacy students.

Martz, S. (Ed.). (1990). *If I had a hammer: Women's work in poetry, fiction, and photography*. Watsonville, CA: Papier-maché Press.

Oresick, P., & Coles, N. (Eds.). (1990). *Working classics: Poems on Industrial life*. Champaign, IL: University of Illinois Press.

This large collection of poetry to be read by and to adult literacy students explores work in the coal mines, canneries, factories, and sweatshops in the United States.

Wayman, T. (Ed.). (1981). *Going for coffee: Poetry on the job*. Madeira Park, BC: Harbour Press.

Wayman, T. (Ed.). (1991). *Paperwork: An anthology*. Madeira Park, BC: Harbour Press.

Wharton, C., & Wayman, T. (Eds.). (1989). *East of Main: An anthology of poems from East Vancouver*. Vancouver, BC: Pulp Press.

Other Useful Collections

Janeczko, P. (Ed.). (1985). *Pocket poems: Selected for a journey*. New York: Bradbury.

A collection of short poems by lesser and more well-known contemporary poets. The topics include meditation on love, war, old age, and the family.

Lipkin, C., & Solotaroff, V. (Eds.). (1990). *Words on the page, the world in your hand*. New York: HarperCollins.

There are three slim volumes in this collection. They include prose and poetry "written, selected, and adapted by contemporary writers for adults in literacy programs and others who wish to expand their reading horizons." We highly recommend this one.

Mazer, N.F., & Lewis, M. (Eds.). (1989). *Waltzing on water: Poetry by women*. New York: Dell.

These short poems are grouped around the topics of being young, friendship, love, mothers and daughters, being women, and growing old.

Prelutsky, J. (Ed.). (1983). *The Random House book of poetry for children*. New York: Random House.

This is a wonderful collection of short poems to be enjoyed by children, parents, and anyone who loves language play. Many of the poems are humorous and likewise employ traditional end rhyme.